A LITTLE HISTORY OF PHILOSOPHY

NIGEL WARBURTON

A LITTLE HISTORY

of

PHILOSOPHY

YALE UNIVERSITY PRESS
NEW HAVEN AND LONDON

For information about this and other Yale University Press publications, please contact:
U.S. Office: sales.press@yale.edu   www.yalebooks.com
Europe Office: sales @yaleup.co.uk   www.yalebooks.co.uk

Set in Minion Pro by IDSUK (DataConnection) Ltd
Printed in Great Britain by TJ International Ltd, Padstow, Cornwall

Library of Congress Cataloging-in-Publication Data

Warburton, Nigel, 1962–
    A little history of philosophy/Nigel Warburton.
        p. cm
    ISBN 978-0-300-15208-1 (cl:alk. paper)
    1. Philosophy—History. 2. Philosophers. I. Title.
    B72.W365 2011

    190—dc22

                                                              2011013537

A catalogue record for this book is available from the British Library.

10 9 8 7 6 5 4

Contents

CHAPTER 1

The Man Who Asked Questions
SOCRATES AND PLATO

About 2,400 years ago in Athens a man was put to death for asking too many questions. There were philosophers before him, but it was with Socrates that the subject really took off. If philosophy has a patron saint, it is Socrates.

Snub-nosed, podgy, shabby and a bit strange, Socrates did not fit in. Although physically ugly and often unwashed, he had great charisma and a brilliant mind. Everyone in Athens agreed that there had never been anyone quite like him and probably wouldn't be again. He was unique. But he was also extremely annoying. He saw himself as one of those horseflies that have a nasty bite – a gadfly. They're irritating, but don't do serious harm. Not everyone in Athens agreed, though. Some loved him; others thought him a dangerous influence.

As a young man he had been a brave soldier fighting in the Peloponnesian wars against the Spartans and their allies. In middle age he shuffled around the marketplace, stopping people from time to time and asking them awkward questions. That was more or less all he did. But the questions he asked were razor-sharp. They seemed straightforward; but they weren't.

An example of this was his conversation with Euthydemus. Socrates asked him whether being deceitful counted as being immoral. Of course it does, Euthydemus replied. He thought that was obvious. But what, Socrates asked, if your friend is feeling very low and might kill himself, and you steal his knife? Isn't that a deceitful act? Of course it is. But isn't it *moral* rather than *immoral* to do that? It's a good thing, not a bad one – despite being a deceitful act. Yes, says Euthydemus, who by now is tied in knots. Socrates by using a clever counter-example has shown that Euthydemus' general comment that being deceitful is immoral doesn't apply in every situation. Euthydemus hadn't realized this before.

Over and over again Socrates demonstrated that the people he met in the marketplace didn't really know what they thought they knew. A military commander would begin a conversation totally confident that he knew what 'courage' meant, but after twenty minutes in Socrates' company would leave completely confused. The experience must have been disconcerting. Socrates loved to reveal the limits of what people genuinely understood, and to question the assumptions on which they built their lives. A conversation that ended in everyone realizing how little they knew was for him a success. Far better that than to carry on believing that you understood something when you didn't.

At that time in Athens the sons of rich men would be sent to study with Sophists. The Sophists were clever teachers who would coach their students in the art of speech-making. They charged very high fees for this. Socrates in contrast didn't charge for his services. In fact he claimed he didn't know anything, so how could he teach at all? This didn't stop students coming to him and listening in on his conversations. It didn't make him popular with the Sophists either.

One day his friend Chaerophon went to the oracle of Apollo at Delphi. The oracle was a wise old woman, a sibyl, who would answer questions that visitors asked. Her answers were usually in the form of a riddle. 'Is anyone wiser than Socrates?' Chaerophon asked. 'No,' came the answer. 'No one is wiser than Socrates.'

When Chaerophon told Socrates about this he didn't believe it at first. It really puzzled him. 'How can I be the wisest man in Athens when I know so little?' he wondered. He devoted years to questioning people to see if anyone was wiser than he was. Finally he realized what the oracle had meant and that she had been right. Lots of people were good at the various things they did – carpenters were good at carpentry, and soldiers knew about fighting. But none of them were truly wise. They didn't really know what they were talking about.

The word 'philosopher' comes from the Greek words meaning 'love of wisdom'. The Western tradition in philosophy, the one that this book follows, spread from Ancient Greece across large parts of the world, at time cross-fertilized by ideas from the East. The kind of wisdom that it values is based on argument, reasoning and asking questions, not on believing things simply because someone important has told you they are true. Wisdom for Socrates was not knowing lots of facts, or knowing how to do something. It meant understanding the true nature of our existence, including the limits of what we can know. Philosophers today are doing more or less what Socrates was doing: asking tough questions, looking at reasons and evidence, struggling to answer some of the most important questions we can ask ourselves about the nature of reality and how we should live. Unlike Socrates, though, modern philosophers have the benefit of nearly two and a half thousand years of philosophical thinking to build on. This book examines ideas of some of the key thinkers writing in this tradition of Western thought, a tradition that Socrates started.

What made Socrates so wise was that he kept asking questions and he was always willing to debate his ideas. Life, he declared, is only worth living if you think about what you are doing. An unexamined existence is all right for cattle, but not for human beings.

Unusually for a philosopher, Socrates refused to write anything down. For him talking was far better than writing. Written words can't answer back; they can't explain anything to you when you don't understand them. Face-to-face conversation was much better, he maintained. In conversation we can take into account the kind of person we are talking to; we can adapt what we say so that the message gets across. Because he refused to write, it's mainly through the work of Socrates' star pupil Plato that we have much idea of what this great man believed and argued about. Plato wrote down a series of conversations between Socrates and the people he questioned. These are known as the Platonic Dialogues and are great works of literature as well as of philosophy – in some ways Plato was the Shakespeare of his day. Reading these dialogues, we get a sense of what Socrates was like, how clever he was and how infuriating.

Actually it isn't even as straightforward as that, as we can't always tell whether Plato was writing down what Socrates really said, or whether he was putting ideas into the mouth of the character he calls 'Socrates', ideas which are Plato's own.

One of the ideas that most people believe is Plato's rather than Socrates' is that the world is not at all as it seems. There is a significant difference between appearance and reality. Most of us mistake appearances for reality. We think we understand, but we don't. Plato believed that only philosophers understand what the world is truly like. They discover the nature of reality by thinking rather than relying on their senses.

To make this point, Plato described a cave. In that imaginary cave there are people chained facing a wall. In front of them they can see flickering shadows that they believe are real things. They aren't. What they see are shadows made by objects held up in front of a fire behind them. These people spend their whole lives thinking that the shadows projected on the wall are the real world. Then one of them breaks free from his chains and turns towards the fire. His eyes are blurry at first, but then he starts to see where he is. He stumbles out of the cave and eventually is able to look at the sun. When he comes back to the cave, no one believes what he has to tell them about the world outside. The man who breaks free is like a philosopher. He sees beyond appearances. Ordinary people have little idea about reality because they are content with looking at what's in front of them rather than thinking deeply about it. But the appearances are deceptive. What they see are shadows, not reality.

This story of the cave is connected with what's come to be known as Plato's Theory of Forms. The easiest way to understand this is through an example. Think of all the circles that you have seen in your life. Was any one of them a perfect circle? No. Not one of them was absolutely perfect. In a perfect circle every point on its circumference is exactly the same distance from the centre point. Real circles never quite achieve this. But you understood what I meant when I used the words 'perfect circle'. So what is that perfect circle? Plato would say that the idea of a perfect circle is the Form of a circle. If you want to understand what a circle is, you should focus on the Form of the circle, not actual circles that you can draw and experience through your visual sense, all of which are imperfect in some way. Similarly, Plato thought, if you want to understand what goodness is, then you need to concentrate on the Form of goodness, not on particular examples of it that you witness. Philosophers are the people who are best suited to thinking about the Forms in this abstract way; ordinary people get led astray by the world as they grasp it through their senses.

Because philosophers are good at thinking about reality, Plato believed they should be in charge and have all the political power. In *The Republic*, his most famous work, he described an imaginary perfect society. Philosophers would be at the top and would get a special education; but they would sacrifice their own pleasures for the sake of the citizens they ruled. Beneath them would be soldiers who were trained to defend the country, and beneath *them* would be the workers. These three groups of people would be in a perfect balance, Plato thought, a balance that was like a well-balanced mind with the reasonable part keeping the emotions and desires in control. Unfortunately his model of society was profoundly anti-democratic, and would keep the people under control by a combination of lies and force. He would have banned most art, on the grounds that he thought it gave false representations of reality. Painters paint appearances, but appearances are deceptive about the Forms. Every aspect of life in Plato's ideal republic would be strictly controlled from above. It's what we would now call a totalitarian state. Plato thought that letting the people vote was like letting the passengers steer a ship – far better to let people who knew what they were doing take charge.

Fifth-century Athens was quite different from the society that Plato imagined in *The Republic*. It was a democracy of sorts, though only about 10 per cent of the population could vote.

Women and slaves, for example, were automatically excluded. But citizens were equal before the law, and there was an elaborate lottery system to make sure that everyone had a fair chance of influencing political decisions.

Athens as a whole didn't value Socrates as highly as Plato valued him. Far from it. Many Athenians felt that Socrates was dangerous and was deliberately undermining the government. In 399 BC, when Socrates was 70 years old, one of them, Meletus, took him to court. He claimed that Socrates was neglecting the Athenian gods, introducing new gods of his own. He also suggested that Socrates was teaching the young men of Athens to behave badly, encouraging them to turn against the authorities. These were both very serious accusations. It is difficult to know now how accurate they were. Perhaps Socrates really did discourage his students from following the state religion, and there is some evidence that he enjoyed mocking Athenian democracy. That would have been consistent with his character. What is certainly true is that many Athenians believed the charges.

They voted on whether or not he was guilty. Just over half of the 501 citizens who made up the huge jury thought he was, and sentenced him to death. If he'd wanted to, he could probably have talked his way out of being executed. But instead, true to his reputation as a gadfly, he annoyed the Athenians even more by arguing that he had done nothing wrong and that they should, in fact, be rewarding him by giving him free meals for life instead of punishing him. That didn't go down well.

He was put to death by being forced to drink poison made from hemlock, a plant that gradually paralyses the body. Socrates said goodbye to his wife and three sons, and then gathered his students around him. If he had the choice to carry on living quietly, not asking any more difficult questions, he would not take it. He'd rather die than that. He had an inner voice that told him to keep questioning everything, and he could not betray it. Then he drank the cup of poison. Very soon he was dead.

In Plato's dialogues, though, Socrates lives on. This difficult man, who kept asking questions and would rather die than stop thinking about how things really are, has been an inspiration for philosophers ever since.

Socrates' immediate impact was on those around him. Plato carried on teaching in the spirit of Socrates after his teacher's death. By far his most impressive pupil was Aristotle, a very different sort of thinker from either of them.

CHAPTER 2

True Happiness
ARISTOTLE

'One swallow doesn't make a summer.' You might think this phrase comes from William Shakespeare or another great poet. It sounds as if it should. In fact it's from Aristotle's book *The Nicomachean Ethics*, so called because he dedicated it to his son Nicomachus. The point he was making was that just as it takes more than the arrival of one swallow to prove that summer has come, and more than a single warm day, so a few moments of pleasure don't add up to true happiness. Happiness for Aristotle wasn't a matter of short-term joy. Surprisingly, he thought that children couldn't be happy. This sounds absurd. If children can't be happy, who can? But it reveals how different his view of happiness was from ours. Children are just beginning their lives, and so haven't had a full life in any sense. True happiness, he argued, required a longer life.

Aristotle was Plato's student, and Plato had been Socrates'. So these three great thinkers form a chain: Socrates–Plato–Aristotle.

This is often the way. Geniuses don't usually emerge from nowhere. Most of them have had an inspirational teacher. But the ideas of these three are very different from each other. They didn't simply parrot what they had been taught. Each had an original approach. Put simply, Socrates was a great talker, Plato was a superb writer, and Aristotle was interested in everything. Socrates and Plato thought of the world we see as a pale reflection of true reality that could only be reached by abstract philosophical thought; Aristotle, in contrast, was fascinated by the details of everything around him.

Unfortunately, almost all the writing by Aristotle that survives is in the form of lecture notes. But these records of his thinking have still made a huge impact on Western philosophy, even if the writing style is often dry. But he wasn't just a philosopher: he was also fascinated by zoology, astronomy, history, politics and drama.

Born in Macedonia in 384 BC, after studying with Plato, travelling, and working as a tutor to Alexander the Great, Aristotle set up his own school in Athens called the Lyceum. This was one of the most famous centres of learning of the Ancient World, a bit like a modern university. From there he sent out researchers who returned with new information about everything from political society to biology. He also started an important library. In a famous Renaissance painting by Raphael, *The School of Athens*, Plato points upwards to the world of the Forms; in contrast, Aristotle is reaching out towards the world in front of him.

Plato would have been content to philosophize from an armchair; but Aristotle wanted to explore the reality we experience through the senses. He rejected his teacher's Theory of Forms, believing instead that the way to understand any general category was to examine particular examples of it. So to understand what a cat is he thought you needed to look at real cats, not think abstractly about the Form of cat.

One question that Aristotle mulled over was 'How should we live?' Socrates and Plato had both asked it before him. The need to answer it is part of what draws people to philosophy in the first place. Aristotle had his own answer. The simple version of it is this: seek happiness.

But what does that phrase 'seek happiness' mean? Today most people told to seek happiness would think of ways they could enjoy themselves. Perhaps happiness for you would involve exotic holidays, going to music festivals or parties, or spending time with friends. It might also mean curling up with your favourite book, or going to an art gallery. But although these might be ingredients in a good life for Aristotle, he certainly didn't believe that the best way to live was to go out and seek pleasure in these ways. That on its own wouldn't be a good life, in his view. The Greek word Aristotle used was *eudaimonia* (pronounced 'you-die-moania', but meaning the opposite). This is sometimes translated as 'flourishing' or 'success' rather than 'happiness'. It is more than the sort of pleasant sensations you can get from eating mango-flavoured ice cream or watching your favourite sports team win. *Eudaimonia* isn't about fleeting moments of bliss or how you feel. It's more objective than that. This is quite hard to grasp as we are so used to thinking that happiness *is* about how we feel and nothing more.

Think of a flower. If you water it, give it enough light, maybe feed it a little, then it will grow and bloom. If you neglect it, keep it in the dark, let insects nibble its leaves, allow it to dry out, it will wilt and die, or at best end up as a very unattractive plant. Human beings can flourish like plants too, though unlike plants we make choices for ourselves: we decide what we want to do and be.

Aristotle was convinced that there is such a thing as human nature, that human beings, as he put it, have a function. There is a way of living that suits us best. What sets us apart from other animals and everything else is that we can think and reason about what we ought to do. From this he concluded that the best kind of life for a human being was one that used our powers of reason.

Surprisingly, Aristotle believed that things you don't know about – and even events after your death – could contribute to your *eudaimonia*. This sounds odd. Assuming there is no after-life, how could anything that happens when you are no longer around affect your happiness? Well, imagine that you are a parent and your happiness in part rests on the hopes for your child's future. If, sadly, that child falls seriously ill after your own death, then your *eudaimonia* will have been affected by this. In Aristotle's view your life will have got worse, even though you won't actually know about your child's sickness and you are no longer alive. This brings out well his idea that happiness is not just a matter of how you feel. Happiness in this sense is your overall achievement in life, something that can be affected by what happens to others you care about. Events outside your control and knowledge affect that. Whether you are happy or not depends partly on good luck.

The central question is: 'What can we do to increase our chance of *eudaimonia*?' Aristotle's answer was: 'Develop the right kind of character.' You need to feel the right kind of emotions at the right time and these will lead you to behave well. In part this will be a matter of how you've been brought up, since the best way to develop good habits is to practise them from an early age. So luck comes in there too. Good patterns of behaviour are virtues; bad ones are vices.

Think of the virtue of bravery in wartime. Perhaps a soldier needs to put his own life at risk in order to save some civilians from an attacking army. A *foolhardy* person has no concern whatsoever for his own safety. He might rush into a dangerous situation too, perhaps even when he does not need to, but that's not true bravery, only reckless risk-taking. At the other extreme, a *cowardly* soldier can't overcome his fear enough to act in an appropriate way at all, and will be paralysed with terror at the very moment when he is most needed. A brave or courageous person in this situation, however, still feels fear, but is able to conquer it and take action. Aristotle thought that every virtue lies in between two extremes like this. Here bravery is halfway between foolhardiness and cowardice. This is sometimes known as Aristotle's doctrine of the Golden Mean.

Aristotle's approach to ethics isn't just of historical interest. Many modern philosophers believe that he was right about the importance of developing the virtues, and that his view of what happiness is was accurate and inspiring. Instead of looking to increase our pleasure in life, they think, we should try to become better people and do the right thing. That is what makes a life go well.

All this makes it sound as if Aristotle was just interested in individual personal development. But he wasn't. Human beings are political animals, he argued. We need to be able to live with other people and we need a system of justice to cope with the darker side of our nature. *Eudaimonia* can only be achieved in relation to life in a society. We live together, and need to find our happiness by interacting well with those around us in a well-ordered political state.

There was one unfortunate side effect of Aristotle's brilliance, though. He was so intelligent, and his research was so thorough, that many who read his work believed he was right about everything. This was bad for progress, and bad for philosophy in the tradition that Socrates had started. For hundreds of years after his death most scholars accepted his views of the world as unquestionably true. If they could prove that Aristotle had said something, that was enough for them. This is what is sometimes called 'truth by authority' – believing something *must* be true because an important 'authority' figure has said it is.

What do you think would happen if you dropped a piece of wood and a piece of heavy metal that was the same size from a high place? Which would hit the ground first? Aristotle thought that the heavier one, the one made of metal, would fall faster. In fact, this isn't what happens. They fall at the same speed. But because Aristotle declared it to be true, throughout the medieval period just about everyone believed that it must be true. No more proof was needed. In the sixteenth century Galileo Galilei supposedly dropped a wooden ball and a cannonball from the leaning tower of Pisa to test this out. Both reached the ground at the same time. So Aristotle was wrong. But it would have been quite easy to show this much earlier.

Relying on someone else's authority was completely against the spirit of Aristotle's research. It's against the spirit of philosophy too. Authority doesn't prove anything by itself. Aristotle's own methods were investigation, research and clear reasoning. Philosophy thrives on debate, on the possibility of being wrong, on challenging views, and exploring alternatives. Fortunately, in most ages there have been philosophers ready to think critically about what other people tell them must be so. One philosopher who tried to think critically about absolutely everything was the sceptic Pyrrho.

CHAPTER 3

We Know Nothing
PYRRHO

No one knows anything – and even that's not certain. You shouldn't rely on what you believe to be true. You might be mistaken. Everything can be questioned, everything doubted. The best option, then, is to keep an open mind. Don't commit, and you won't be disappointed. That was the main teaching of Scepticism, a philosophy that was popular for several hundred years in Ancient Greece and later in Rome. Unlike Plato and Aristotle, the most extreme sceptics avoided holding firm opinions on anything whatsoever. The Ancient Greek Pyrrho (*c.* 365–*c.* 270 BC) was the most famous and probably the most extreme sceptic of all time. His life was decidedly odd.

You may believe that you know all kinds of things. You know that you are reading this now, for example. But sceptics would challenge this. Think about why you believe that you are actually reading this and not just imagining that you are. Can you be sure that you are right? You appear to be reading – that's the way it seems to you. But perhaps you are hallucinating or dreaming (this is an idea that René Descartes would develop some eighteen hundred years later: see Chapter 11). Socrates' insistence that all that he knew was how little he knew was a sceptical position too. But Pyrrho took it much much further. He probably took it a little too far.

If reports of his life are to be believed (and perhaps we should be sceptical about *them* too), Pyrrho made a career from not taking anything for granted. Like Socrates, he never wrote anything down. So what we know about him comes from what other people recorded, mostly several centuries after his death. One of those, Diogenes Laertius, tells us that Pyrrho became a celebrity and was made a high priest of Elis where he lived and that in his honour philosophers didn't have to pay any taxes. We have no way of checking the truth of this, though it does sound like a good idea.

As far as we can tell, though, Pyrrho lived out his scepticism in some quite extraordinary ways. His time on earth would have been very short if he hadn't had friends to protect him. Any extreme sceptic needs the support of less sceptical people, or very good luck, to survive for long.

Here's how he approached life. We can't completely trust the senses. Sometimes they mislead us. It's easy to make a mistake about what you can see in the dark, for example. What looks like a fox may only be a cat. Or you might think you heard someone calling you when it was only the wind in the trees. Because our senses quite often mislead us, Pyrrho decided *never* to trust them. He didn't rule out the possibility that they might be giving him accurate information, but he kept an open mind on the issue.

So, whereas most people would take the sight of a cliff edge with a sheer drop as strong evidence that it would be very foolish to keep walking forward, Pyrrho didn't. His senses might be deceiving him, so he didn't trust them. Even the feeling of his toes curling over the cliff edge, or the sensation of tipping forward, wouldn't have convinced him he was about to fall to the rocks below. It wasn't even obvious to him that falling on to rocks would be so bad for his health. How could he be absolutely sure of that? His friends, who presumably weren't all Sceptics themselves, stopped him having accidents, but if they hadn't, he would have been in trouble every few minutes.

Why be afraid of savage dogs if you can't be sure they want to hurt you? Just because they're barking and baring their teeth and running towards you doesn't mean they'll definitely bite. And even if they do, it won't *necessarily* hurt. Why care about oncoming traffic when you cross the road? Those carts might not hit you. Who really knows? And what difference does it make if you are alive or dead anyway? Somehow Pyrrho managed to live out this philosophy of total indifference and conquer all the usual and natural human emotions and patterns of behaviour.

That's the legend anyway. Some of these stories about him were probably invented to make fun of his philosophy. But it's unlikely that they're all fictional. For example, he famously kept completely calm while sailing through one of the worst storms anyone had ever witnessed. The wind was tearing the sails to pieces and huge waves were breaking over the ship. Everyone around him was terrified. But it didn't bother Pyrrho in the least. Since appearances are so often deceptive, he couldn't be absolutely sure that any harm would come from it. He managed to remain peaceful while even the most experienced sailors were panicking. He demonstrated that it's possible to stay indifferent even under these conditions. That story has a ring of truth about it.

As a young man, Pyrrho visited India. Perhaps that was what inspired him in his unusual lifestyle. India has a great tradition of spiritual teachers or gurus putting themselves through extreme and almost unbelievable physical deprivation: being buried alive, hanging weights from sensitive parts of their bodies, or living for weeks without food, to achieve inner stillness. Pyrrho's approach to philosophy was certainly close to that of a mystic. Whatever techniques he used to achieve this, he certainly practised what he preached. His calm state of mind made a deep impression on those around him. The reason he didn't get worked up about anything was that, in his opinion, absolutely everything was simply a matter of opinion. If there's no chance of discovering the truth, then there's no need to fret. We can then distance ourselves from all firm beliefs, because firm beliefs always involve delusion.

If you'd met Pyrrho, you'd probably have thought he was mad. And perhaps he was in a way. But his views and his behaviour were consistent. He would think that your various certainties were simply unreasonable and stood in the way of your peace of mind. You are taking too much for granted. It's as if you have built a house on sand. The foundations of your thought aren't anything like as firm as you'd like to believe and are unlikely to make you happy.

Pyrrho neatly summarized his philosophy in the form of three questions anyone who wants to be happy should ask:

What are things really like?
What attitude should we adopt to them?
What will happen to someone who does adopt that attitude?

His answers were simple and to the point. First, we can't ever know what the world is really like – that's beyond us. No one will ever know about the ultimate nature of reality. Such knowledge simply isn't possible for human beings. So forget about that. This view is completely at odds with Plato's Theory of Forms and the possibility that philosophers could gain knowledge of them through abstract thought (see Chapter 1). Secondly, and as a result of this, we shouldn't commit to any view. Because we can't know anything for sure, we should suspend all judgement and live our lives in an uncommitted way. Every desire that you have suggests that you believe that one thing is better than another. Unhappiness arises from not getting what you want. But you can't know that anything is better than anything else. So, he thought, to be happy you should free yourself from desires and not care about how things turn out. That is the right way to live. Recognize that nothing matters. That way nothing will affect your state of mind, which will be one of inner tranquillity. Thirdly, if you follow this teaching this is what will happen to you. You will start off by being speechless, presumably because you won't know what to say about anything. Eventually, you will be free from all worry. That's the best you or anyone can hope for in life. It's almost like a religious experience.

That's the theory. It seemed to work for Pyrrho, though it is hard to see it giving the same results for most of humanity. Few of us will ever achieve the kind of indifference that he recommended. And not everyone will be lucky enough to have a team of friends to save them from their worst mistakes. In fact, if everyone followed his advice, there wouldn't be anyone left to protect the Pyrrhonic Sceptics from themselves and the whole school of philosophy would very quickly die out as they toppled over cliff edges, stepped in front of moving vehicles, or were savaged by vicious dogs.

The basic weakness of Pyrrho's approach is that he moved from 'You can't know anything' to the conclusion 'Therefore you should ignore your instincts and feelings about what is dangerous'. But our instincts do save us from many possible dangers. They may not be totally reliable, but that doesn't mean we should just ignore them. Even Pyrrho is supposed to have moved away when a dog snapped at him: he couldn't completely overcome his automatic reactions however much he wanted to. So to try and live out Pyrrhonic Scepticism seems perverse. Nor is it obvious that living this way produces the peace of mind that Pyrrho thought it would. It is possible to be sceptical about Pyrrho's Scepticism. You might want to question whether tranquillity really will come from taking the sorts of risks that he took. It might have worked for Pyrrho, but what is the evidence that it will work for you? You might not be 100 per cent sure that a ferocious dog will bite you, but it makes sense not to take the chance if it is 99 per cent certain.

Not all sceptics in the history of philosophy have been as extreme as Pyrrho. There is a great tradition of moderate scepticism, of questioning assumptions and looking closely at the evidence for what we believe, without attempting to live as if everything was in doubt all of the time. Sceptical questioning of this sort is at the heart of philosophy. All the great philosophers have been sceptics in this sense. It is the opposite of dogmatism. Someone who is dogmatic is very confident that they know the truth. Philosophers challenge dogma. They ask why people believe what they do, what sorts of evidence they have to support their conclusions. That was what Socrates and Aristotle did and it is what present-day philosophers do too. But they don't do this just for the sake of being difficult. The point of moderate philosophical scepticism is to get closer to the truth, or at least to reveal how little we know or can know. You don't need to risk falling off a cliff edge to be this kind of sceptic. But you do need to be prepared to ask awkward questions and to think critically about the answers that people give you.

Although Pyrrho preached freedom from all cares, most of us don't achieve that. One common worry is the fact that each of us will die. Another Greek philosopher, Epicurus, had some clever suggestions about how we can come to terms with this.

CHAPTER 4

The Garden Path
EPICURUS

Imagine your funeral. What will it be like? Who'll be there? What will they say? What you are imagining must be from your own perspective. It's as if you are still there watching events from a particular place, perhaps from above, or from a seat among the mourners. Now, some people do believe that that is a serious possibility, that after death we can survive outside a physical body as a kind of spirit that might even be able to see what's going on in this world. But for those of us who believe death is final, there is a real problem. Every time we try and imagine not being there we have to do it by imagining that we *are* there, watching what is happening when we're not there.

Whether or not you can imagine your own death, it seems quite natural to be at least a bit afraid of not existing. Who wouldn't fear their own death? If there's anything we should be anxious about, it's surely that. It seems perfectly reasonable to worry about not existing even if that will happen many years from now. It's instinctive. Very few people alive have *never* thought deeply about this.

The Ancient Greek philosopher Epicurus (341–270 BC) argued that fear of death was a waste of time and based on bad logic. It was a state of mind to be overcome. If you think clearly about it, death shouldn't be frightening at all. Once you get your thinking straight you'll enjoy your time here much more – which for Epicurus was extremely important. The point of philosophy, he believed, was to make your life go better, to help you find happiness. Some people believe that it is morbid to dwell on your own death, but for Epicurus it was a way of making living more intense.

Epicurus was born on the Greek island of Samos in the Aegean. He spent most of his life in Athens where he became something of a cult figure, attracting a group of students who lived with him in a commune. The group included women and slaves – a rare situation in Ancient Athens. This didn't make him popular, except with his followers who almost worshipped him. He ran this philosophy school in a house with a garden – and so it came to be known as The Garden.

Like many Ancient philosophers (and some modern ones, such as Peter Singer: see Chapter 40), Epicurus believed that philosophy should be practical. It should change how you live. So it was important that those who joined him in The Garden put the philosophy into practice rather than just learnt about it.

For Epicurus the key to life was recognizing that we all seek pleasure. More importantly, we avoid pain whenever we can. That's what drives us. Eliminating suffering from your life and increasing happiness will make it go better. The best way to live, then, was this: have a very simple lifestyle, be kind to those around you, and surround yourself with friends. That way you'll be able to satisfy most of your desires. You won't be left wanting something you can't get. It's no good having a desperate urge to own a mansion if you won't ever have the money to buy one. Don't spend your whole life working in order to get something that is probably beyond your reach anyway. It's far better to live in a simple way. If your desires are simple they are easy to satisfy and you will have the time and energy to enjoy the things that matter. That was his recipe for happiness, and it makes a lot of sense.

This teaching was a form of therapy. Epicurus' aim was to cure his students of mental pain, and to suggest how physical pain could be made bearable by remembering past pleasures. He pointed out that pleasures are enjoyable at the time, but they are also enjoyable when we remember them afterwards, so they can have long-lasting benefits for us. When he was dying and in some discomfort, he wrote to a friend about how he managed to distract himself from his illness by recalling his enjoyment of their past conversations.

This is all quite different from what the word 'epicurean' means today. It's almost the opposite. An 'epicure' is someone who loves eating fine foods, someone who indulges in luxury and sensual pleasure. Epicurus had much simpler tastes than that suggests. He taught the need to be moderate – giving in to greedy appetites would just create more and more desires and so in the end produce the mental anguish of unfulfilled craving. That sort of life of wanting more and more should be avoided. He and his followers ate bread and water rather than exotic food. If you start drinking expensive wine, then you'll very soon end up wanting to drink even more expensive wine, and get caught in the trap of longing for things that you can't have. Despite this, his enemies claimed that in The Garden commune Epicureans spent most of their time eating, drinking and having sex with each other in a non-stop orgy. That's how the modern meaning of 'epicurean' got going. If Epicurus' followers really did do this, it was completely at odds with their leader's teaching. It's more likely, though, that this was just a malicious rumour.

One thing Epicurus certainly did spend a lot of time doing was writing. He was prolific. Records suggest that he wrote as many as three hundred books on rolls of papyrus, though none of these has survived. What we know about him comes mostly from notes followers wrote. They learnt his books by heart, but they also passed on his teaching in written form. Some of their scrolls survived in fragments, preserved in the volcanic ash that fell on Herculaneum near Pompeii when Mount Vesuvius erupted. Another important source of information about Epicurus' teaching is the long poem *On the Nature of Things* by the Roman philosopher-poet, Lucretius. Composed over two hundred years after Epicurus' death, this poem summarized the key teachings of his school.

So, to return to the question that Epicurus asked, why shouldn't you fear death? One reason is that you won't experience it. Your death won't be something that happens to *you*. When it happens you won't be there. The twentieth-century philosopher Ludwig Wittgenstein echoed this view when he wrote in his *Tractatus Logico-Philosophicus*, 'Death is not an event in life'. The idea here is that events are things that we experience, but our own death is the removal of the possibility of experience, not something further that we could be conscious of and somehow live through.

When we imagine our own death, Epicurus suggested, most of us make the mistake of thinking there will be something of us left to feel whatever happens to the dead body. But this is a misunderstanding about what we are. We are tied to our particular bodies, our particular flesh and bone. Epicurus' view was that we consist of atoms (though what he meant by this term was a bit different from what modern scientists mean by it). Once these atoms come apart at death we no longer exist as individuals capable of consciousness. Even if someone could carefully put all the bits back together again later, and breathe life back into this reconstructed body, it wouldn't be anything to do with *me*. The new living body wouldn't be me, despite looking like me. I wouldn't feel its pains, because once the body ceases to function nothing can bring it back to life. The chain of identity would have been broken.

Another way Epicurus thought he could cure his followers of their fear of death was by pointing out the difference between what we feel about the future and what we feel about the past. We care about one but not the other. Think about the time before your birth. There was all that time that you didn't exist. Not just the weeks when you were in your mother's womb when you might have been born early, or even the point before you were conceived but were just a possibility for your parents, but rather the trillions of years before you came along. We don't usually worry about not existing for all those millennia before our birth. Why should anyone care about all that time that they didn't exist? But then, if that's true, why should we care so much about all those aeons of non-existence after death? Our thought is asymmetrical. We're very biased towards worrying about the time after our death rather than the time before our birth. But Epicurus thought this was a mistake. Once you see this, you should start thinking of the time after your death in the same sort of way that you do the time before it. Then it won't be a big concern.

Some people get very worried that they might end up being punished in an afterlife. Epicurus dismissed that worry too. The gods aren't really interested in their creation, he confidently told his followers. They exist apart from us, and don't get involved with the world. So you should be all right. That's the cure – the combination of these arguments. If it works, you should feel much more relaxed about your future non-existence now. Epicurus summed up his whole philosophy in his epitaph:

'I was not; I have been; I am not; I do not mind'

If you believe that we are simply physical beings, composed of matter, and that there is no serious risk of punishment after death, then Epicurus' reasoning may well persuade you that your death is nothing to be afraid of. You might still worry about the process of dying as that is often painful and definitely experienced. That's true even if it is unreasonable to fret about death itself. Remember, though, that Epicurus believed that good memories could ease pain, so he had an answer even for that. But if you think that you are a soul in a body, and that soul can survive bodily death, Epicurus' cure is unlikely to work for you: you will be able to imagine carrying on existing even after your heart has stopped beating.

The Epicureans weren't alone in thinking of philosophy as a type of therapy: most Greek and Roman philosophers did. The Stoics, in particular, were renowned for their lessons in how to be psychologically tough in the face of unfortunate events.

CHAPTER 5

Learning Not to Care
EPICTETUS, CICERO, SENECA

If it starts to rain just as you have to leave your house, that is unfortunate. But if you have to go out, apart from putting on a raincoat or getting your umbrella, or cancelling your appointment, there isn't much you can do about it. You can't stop the rain no matter how much you want to. Should you be upset about this? Or should you just be philosophical? 'Being philosophical' simply means accepting what you can't change. What about the inevitable process of growing older and the shortness of life? How should you feel about these features of the human condition? Same again?

When people say they are 'philosophical' about what happens to them, they are using the word as the Stoics would have done. The name 'Stoic' came from the Stoa, which was a painted porch in Athens where these philosophers used to meet. One of the first was Zeno of Citium (334–262 BC). Early Greek Stoics had views on a wide range of philosophical problems about reality, logic and ethics. But they were most famous for their views on mental control. Their basic idea was that we should only worry about things we can change. We shouldn't get worked up about anything else. Like the Sceptics, they aimed for a calm state of mind. Even when facing tragic events, such as the death of a loved one, the Stoic should remain unmoved. Our *attitude* to what happens is within our control even though *what* happens often isn't.

At the heart of Stoicism was the idea that we are responsible for what we feel and think. We can choose our response to good and bad luck. Some people think of their emotions as like the weather. The Stoics, in contrast, thought that what we feel about a situation or event is a matter of choice. Emotions don't simply happen to us. We don't have to feel sad when we fail to get what we want; we don't have to feel angry when someone tricks us. They believed emotions clouded reasoning and damaged judgement. We should not just control them, but wherever possible remove them altogether.

Epictetus (AD 55–135), one of the best-known later Stoics, started out as a slave. He had endured many hardships and knew about pain and hunger – he walked with a limp as a result of a bad beating. When he declared that the mind can remain free even when the body is enslaved he was drawing on his own experience. This wasn't just an abstract theory. His teaching included practical advice about how to deal with pain and suffering. It boiled down to this: 'Our thoughts are up to us.' This philosophy inspired a US fighter pilot James B. Stockdale who was shot down over North Vietnam during the Vietnam war. Stockdale was tortured many times and kept in a cell in solitary confinement for four years. He managed to survive by applying what he remembered of Epictetus' teaching from a course he had taken in college. As he drifted down towards enemy territory on his parachute he resolved to stay unmoved by what others did to him, no matter how harsh his treatment. If he couldn't change it, he wouldn't let it affect him. Stoicism gave him the strength to survive the pain and loneliness that would have destroyed most people.

This tough philosophy began in Ancient Greece, but it was in the Roman Empire that it flourished. Two important writers who helped to spread the Stoic teaching were Marcus Tullius Cicero (106–43 BC) and Lucius Annaeus Seneca (1 BC–AD 65). The brevity of life and the inevitably of ageing were topics that particularly interested them. They recognized that ageing is a natural process, and didn't try to change what couldn't be changed. At the same time, though, they believed in making the best of our short time here.

Cicero seemed to pack more than most into a day: he was a lawyer and politician as well as a philosopher. In his book *On Old Age* he identified four main problems with growing older: it gets harder to work, the body becomes weaker, joy in physical pleasures goes, and death is close. Ageing is inevitable but, as Cicero argued, we can choose how we react to that process. We should recognize that decline in old age need not make life unbearable. First, old people can often get by doing less because of their experience, so any work they do can be more effective. Their bodies and minds won't necessarily decline dramatically if they exercise them. And even if physical pleasures become less enjoyable, old people can spend more time on friendship and conversation which are themselves very rewarding. Finally, he believed that the soul lived for ever, so that old people shouldn't worry about dying. Cicero's attitude was that we should both accept the natural process of growing older and recognize that the attitude we take to that process need not be pessimistic.

Seneca, another great popularizer of Stoic views, took a similar line when he wrote about the brevity of life. You don't often hear people complaining that life is too long. Most say it's far too short. There's so much to do and so little time in which to do it. In the words of the Ancient Greek Hippocrates, 'Life is short, art is long.' Old people who can see their death approaching often wish for just a few more years so that they can achieve what they really wanted to in life. But often it's too late and they're left feeling sad about what might have been. Nature is cruel in this respect. Just as we are getting on top of things, we die.

Seneca didn't agree with this view. An all-rounder like Cicero, he found time to be a playwright, a politician and a successful businessman as well as a philosopher. The problem as he saw it was not how short our lives are, but rather how badly most of us use what time we have. Once again, it was our attitude to unavoidable aspects of the human condition that mattered most for him. We should not feel angry that life is short, but instead should make the most of it. He pointed out that some people would waste a thousand years as easily as they do the life that they have. And even then they'd probably still complain that life was too short. In fact life is usually long enough to get plenty done if we make the right choices: if we don't fritter it away on useless tasks. Some chase after money with such energy that they don't have time to do much else; others fall into the trap of giving over all their free time to drinking and sex.

If you wait till you are old to discover this, it will be too late, Seneca thought. Having white hair and wrinkles doesn't guarantee that an old person has spent much time doing anything worthwhile, even though some people mistakenly act as if it does. Someone who sets sail in a ship and is carried this way and that by stormy winds hasn't been on a voyage. He's just been tossed about a lot. So it is with life. Being out of control, drifting through events without finding time for the experiences that are most valuable and meaningful, is very different from truly living.

One benefit of living your life well is that you won't have to be afraid of your memories when you are old. If you waste your time, when you look back you may not want to think about how you spent your life, as it will probably be too painful to contemplate all the opportunities you missed. That's why so many people become preoccupied with trivial work, Seneca thought – it's a way of avoiding the truth about what they've failed to do. He urged his readers to remove themselves from the crowd and to avoid hiding from themselves by being busy.

How, then, according to Seneca, *should* we spend our time? The Stoic ideal was to live like a recluse, away from other people. The most fruitful way to exist, he declared – perceptively – was studying philosophy. This was a way of being truly alive.

Seneca's life gave him plenty of chances to practise what he preached. In AD 41, for example, he was accused of having an affair with the Emperor Gaius' sister. It's not clear whether he had or not, but the result was that he was sent into exile in Corsica for the next eight years. Then his luck turned again and he was called back to Rome to become tutor to the 12-year-old emperor-to-be, Nero. Later Seneca acted as his speechwriter and political advisor. This relationship ended very badly, though: another twist of fate. Nero accused Seneca of being part of a plot to murder him. There was no escape for Seneca this time. Nero told him to commit suicide. Refusal was out of the question and would have led to execution anyway. To resist would have been pointless. He took his own life, and, true to his Stoicism, was peaceful and calm to the end.

One way of looking at the main teaching of the Stoics is to think of it as a kind of psychotherapy, a series of psychological techniques that will make our lives calmer. Get rid of those troublesome emotions that cloud your thinking and everything will be much more straightforward. Unfortunately, though, even if you manage to calm your emotions, you may find that you have lost something important. The state of indifference championed by the Stoics may reduce unhappiness in the face of events we can't control. But the cost might be that we become cold, heartless, and perhaps even less human. If that is the price of achieving calm, it may be too high.

Although influenced by Ancient Greek philosophy, Augustine, an early Christian whose ideas we'll turn to next, was far from a Stoic. He was a man of strong passions with a deep concern about the evil he saw in the world and a desperate desire to understand God and his plans for humanity.

CHAPTER 6

Who Is Pulling Our Strings?
AUGUSTINE

Augustine (354–430) desperately wanted to know the truth. As a Christian, he believed in God. But his belief left many questions unanswered. What did God want him to do? How should he live? What should he believe? He spent most of his waking life thinking and writing about these questions. The stakes were very high. For people who believe in the possibility of spending eternity in hell, making a philosophical mistake can seem to have terrible consequences. As Augustine saw it, he might end up burning in sulphur for ever if he was wrong. One problem he agonized over was why God allowed evil in the world. The answer he gave is still a popular one with many believers.

In the medieval period, roughly from the fifth to the fifteenth century, philosophy and religion were very tightly interlinked. Medieval philosophers learnt from Ancient Greek philosophers such as Plato and Aristotle. But they adapted their ideas, applying them to their own religions. Many of these philosophers were

Christians, but there were important Jewish and Arabic philosophers such as Maimonides and Avicenna too. Augustine, who was much later made a saint, stands out as one of the greatest.

Augustine was born in Tagaste in what is now Algeria in North Africa but was then still part of the Roman Empire. His real name was Aurelius Augustinus, though he is now almost always known as either St Augustine or Augustine of Hippo (after the city where he later lived).

Augustine's mother was a Christian, but his father followed a local religion. After a wild youth and early adulthood during which he had a child by a mistress, Augustine converted to Christianity in his thirties, eventually becoming Bishop of Hippo. He famously asked God to make him stop having sexual desires 'but not yet', because he was enjoying worldly pleasures too much. In later life he wrote many books including his *Confessions, The City of God* and almost a hundred others, drawing heavily on the wisdom of Plato but giving it a Christian twist.

Most Christians think that God has special powers: he or she is supremely good, knows everything and can do anything. That is all part of the definition of 'God'. God wouldn't be God without having these qualities. In many other religions God is described in similar ways, but Augustine was only interested in a Christian perspective.

Anyone who believes in this God will still have to admit there is a great deal of suffering in the world. That would be very hard to deny. Some is the result of natural evil such as earthquakes and diseases. Some of this suffering is due to moral evil: evil caused by human beings. Murder and torture are two obvious examples of moral evil. Long before Augustine was writing, the Greek philosopher Epicurus (see Chapter 4) had recognized that this presents a problem. How could a good, all-powerful God tolerate evil? If God can't stop it happening, then he can't be truly all-powerful. There are limits to what he can do. But if God *is* all-powerful and doesn't seem inclined to stop it, how can he be all-good? That didn't seem to make sense. It puzzles many people today too. Augustine focused on moral evil. He realized that the idea of a good God who knows that this kind of evil happens and does nothing to prevent it is difficult to understand. He wasn't satisfied with the idea that God moves in mysterious ways that are beyond human comprehension. Augustine wanted answers.

Imagine a murderer about to kill his victim. He is poised over him with a sharp knife. A truly evil act is about to take place. Yet we know that God is powerful enough to stop it happening. It would just take a few minor alterations to the neurons in the would-be murderer's brain. Or God could makes knives turn soft and rubbery every time someone tried to use them as a deadly weapon. That way they would just bounce off the victim, and no one would get hurt. God must know what's going on as he knows absolutely everything. Nothing can escape him. And he must want the evil not to happen, because that is part of what it means to be supremely good. Yet the murderer kills his victim all the same. Steel knives don't turn to rubber. There is no flash of lightning, no thunderbolt, the weapon doesn't miraculously fall from the murderer's hand. Nor does the murderer change his mind at the last minute. So what is going on? This is the classic Problem of Evil, the problem of explaining why God allows such things. Presumably if everything comes from God, then the evil must come from God too. In some sense God must have wanted this to happen.

In his younger days Augustine had a way of avoiding believing that God wanted evil to happen. He was a Manichaean. Manichaeism was a religion that originally came from Persia (present-day Iran). The Manichaeans believed that God wasn't supremely powerful. Instead there was a never-ending struggle going on between equal forces of good and evil. So on this view, God and Satan were locked in an ongoing battle for control. Both were immensely strong, but neither was powerful enough to defeat the other. In particular places at particular times, evil got the upper hand. But never for long. Goodness would return and triumph over evil again. This explained why such terrible things happened. Evil came from dark forces and goodness from the forces of light.

Within a person, the Manichaeans believed, goodness came from the soul. Evil came from the body, with all its weaknesses and desires and its tendency to lead us astray. This explained why people were sometimes drawn towards wrongdoing. The problem of evil wasn't such a problem for them because the Manichaeans didn't accept the idea that God was so powerful that he controlled every aspect of reality. If God didn't have power over everything, then he wasn't responsible for the existence of evil, nor could anyone blame God for failing to prevent evil. Manichaeans would have explained the murderer's actions as due to the powers of darkness within him leading him towards evil. These powers were so strong in an individual that the forces of light could not defeat them.

In later life Augustine came to reject the Manichaean approach. He couldn't see why the struggle between good and evil would be never-ending. Why didn't God win the battle? Surely the forces of good were stronger than those of evil? Although Christians accept that there can be powers of evil, these powers are never as strong as God's power. Yet if God was truly all-powerful, as Augustine came to believe, the problem of evil remained. Why *did* God allow evil? Why was there so much of it? There was no easy solution. Augustine thought long and hard about these problems. His main solution was based on the existence of free will: the human ability to choose what we will do next. It's often known as the Free Will Defence. This is theodicy – the attempt to explain and defend how a good God could allow suffering.

God has given us free will. You can, for example choose whether or not to read the next sentence. That's your choice. If no one is forcing you to read on, then you are free to stop. Augustine thought having free will is good. It allows us to act morally. We can decide to be good, which for him meant following God's commands, particularly the Ten Commandments, as well as Jesus' command to 'Love thy neighbour'. But a consequence of having free will is that we can decide to do evil. We can be led astray and do bad things, like lying, stealing, harming or even killing people. This often happens when our emotions overpower our reason. We develop strong desires for objects and for money. We give in to our physical lusts and are led away from God and what God commands. Augustine believed that the rational side of us should keep our passions under control, a view he shared with Plato. Human beings, unlike animals, have the power of reason and should use it. If God had programmed us always to choose good over evil we wouldn't do any harm, but we wouldn't really be free, and we couldn't use our reason to decide what to do. God could have made us like that. Augustine argued that it was much better that he gave us choice. Otherwise we'd have been like puppets with God pulling all our strings so that we always behaved ourselves. There would be no point in thinking about how to behave since we would always automatically choose the good option.

So God is powerful enough to prevent all evil. But the fact that evil exists is still not directly due to God. Moral evil is a result of our choices. Augustine believed that it was also partly a result of Adam and Eve's choices. Like many Christians of his time, he was convinced that things went terribly wrong in the Garden of Eden as described in the first book of the Bible, Genesis. When Eve and then Adam ate from the Tree of Knowledge and so betrayed God, they brought sin into the world. This sin, called Original Sin, was not just something that affected their lives. Absolutely every human being pays the price. Augustine believed that Original Sin gets passed on to each new generation by the act of sexual reproduction. Even a child from its earliest moments bears traces of this sin. Original Sin makes us more likely to sin ourselves.

For many present-day readers, this idea that we are somehow to blame and are being punished for actions that someone else committed is very hard to accept. It seems unfair. But the idea that evil is the result of our having free will and not directly due to God still convinces many believers – it allows them to believe in an all-knowing, all-powerful and all-good God.

Boethius, one of the most popular writers of the Middle Ages, believed in such a God, but he wrestled with a different issue about free will: the question of how we could choose to do anything if God already knows what we'll choose.

CHAPTER 7

The Consolation of Philosophy
BOETHIUS

If you were in prison awaiting execution would you spend your last days writing a philosophy book? Boethius did. It turned out to be the most popular book that he wrote.

Ancius Manlius Severinus Boethius (475–525), to give him his full name, was one of the last Roman philosophers. He died just twenty years before Rome fell to the barbarians. But in his lifetime Rome was already going downhill. Like his fellow Romans Cicero and Seneca, he thought of philosophy as a kind of self-help, a practical way of making your life go better as well as a discipline of abstract thought. He also provided a link back to the Ancient Greeks Plato and Aristotle whose work he translated into Latin, keeping their ideas alive at a time when there was a risk that they might be lost for ever. As a Christian, his writing appealed to the devoutly religious philosophers who read his books in the Middle Ages. His philosophy, then, made a bridge from Greek and Roman thinkers forward to the

Christian philosophy that would dominate the West for centuries after his death.

Boethius' life was a mixture of good and bad luck. King Theodoric, a Goth who ruled Rome at the time, gave him the high office of Consul. He made Boethius' sons consuls too as a special honour, even though they were too young to have got there by their own merit. Everything seemed to be going right for him. He was rich, from a good family, and showered with praise. Somehow he managed to find time for his philosophical studies alongside his work for the government, and he was a prolific writer and translator. He was having a great time. But then his luck changed. Accused of plotting against Theodoric, he was sent away from Rome to Ravenna where he was held in prison, tortured and then executed by a combination of strangulation and being beaten to death. He always maintained that he was innocent, but his accusers didn't believe him.

While in prison, knowing that he was soon to die, Boethius wrote a book that, after his death, became a medieval bestseller, *The Consolation of Philosophy*. It opens with Boethius in his prison cell feeling sorry for himself. Suddenly he realizes that there is a woman looking down at him. Her height seems to change from average to higher than the sky. She is wearing a torn dress embroidered with a ladder that rises from the Greek letter pi at the hem up to the letter theta. In one hand she holds a sceptre, in the other books. This woman turns out to be Philosophy. When she speaks, she tells Boethius what he should believe. She is angry with him for forgetting about her, and has come to remind him how he should be reacting to what has happened to him. The rest of the book is their conversation, which is all about luck and God. It is written partly in prose and partly in poetry. The woman, Philosophy, gives him advice.

She tells Boethius that luck always changes, and that he shouldn't be surprised by this. That's the nature of luck. It is fickle. The wheel of Fortune turns. Sometimes you are at the top; sometimes you are at the bottom. A wealthy king can find himself in poverty in a day. Boethius should realize that's just the way it is. Luck is random. There is no guarantee that because you are lucky today you will be lucky tomorrow.

Mortals, Philosophy explains, are foolish to let their happiness depend on something so changeable. True happiness can only come from inside, from the things that human beings can control, not from anything that bad luck can destroy. This is the Stoic position that we looked at in Chapter 5. When people describe themselves as 'philosophical' about bad things happening to them today, this is what they mean; they try not to be affected by things outside their control, like the weather or who their parents are. Nothing, Philosophy tells Boethius, is terrible in itself – it all depends on how you think about it. Happiness is a state of mind, not of the world, an idea Epictetus would have recognized as his own.

Philosophy wants Boethius to turn once again to her. She tells him he can be truly happy despite being in prison waiting to be killed. She is going to cure him of his distress. The message is that riches, power and honour are worthless since they can come and go. No one should base their happiness on such fragile foundations. Happiness has to come from something that is more solid, something that can't be taken away. As Boethius believed that he would continue to live after death, seeking happiness in trivial worldly things was a mistake. He would lose them all at death anyway.

But where can Boethius find true happiness? Philosophy's answer is that he will find it in God or goodness (these turn out to be the same thing). Boethius was an early Christian, but doesn't mention this in *The Consolation of Philosophy*. The God that Philosophy describes could be Plato's God, the pure Form of goodness. But later readers would recognize Christian teaching about the worthlessness of honour and riches, and the importance of focusing on pleasing God.

Throughout the book Philosophy reminds Boethius of what he already knows. That is again something that comes from Plato, since Plato believed that all learning is really a kind of recollection of ideas we already have. We never really learn anything new, just have our memories jogged. Life is a struggle to recall what we knew earlier. What Boethius already knows at some level is that he was wrong to worry about his loss of freedom and public respect. Those are largely outside his control. What matters is his attitude to his situation, and that is something he can choose.

But Boethius is puzzled by a genuine problem that has worried many people who believe in God. God, being perfect, must know everything that has happened, but also everything that will happen. That is what we mean when we describe God as 'all-knowing'. So if God exists, he must know who will win the next World Cup, and what I'm going to write next. He must have foreknowledge of everything that will ever happen. What he foresees must necessarily happen. So at this moment God knows how everything will turn out.

It follows from all this that God must know what I'm going to do next, even if I'm not yet sure what that will be. At the time when I make a decision about what to do, different possible futures seem to lie open to me. If I come to a fork in the road, I can go left or right, or perhaps just sit down. I could at this moment stop writing and go and make myself some coffee. Or else I can choose to carry on typing on my laptop. That feels like my decision, something I can choose to do or not do. No one is forcing me one way or the other. Similarly, you could choose to close your eyes now if you wanted to. How can that be when God knows what we'll end up doing?

If God already knows what we are both going to do, how can either of us have a genuine choice about what we are going to do? Is choice just an illusion? It seems that I can't have free will if God knows everything. Ten minutes ago God could have written on a piece of paper, 'Nigel will carry on writing.' It was true then, and so I necessarily would carry on writing, whether or not I realized this at the time. But if he could have done that, then surely I didn't have a choice about what I did, even though it felt as if I did. My life was already mapped out for me in every tiniest detail. And if we don't have any choice about our actions, how is it fair to punish or reward us for what we do? If we can't choose what to do, then how can God decide whether or not we shall go to heaven?

This is very perplexing. It is what philosophers call a paradox. It does not seem possible that someone could know what I am going to do and that I would still have free choice about what I do. These two ideas seem to contradict each other. Yet both are plausible if you believe that God is all-knowing.

But Philosophy, the woman in Boethius' cell, has some answers. We do have free will, she tells him. That isn't an illusion. Although God knows what we will do, our lives aren't predestined. Or to put it another way, God's knowledge of what we will do is different from predestination (the idea that we have no choice about what we will do). We do still have a choice about what to do next. The mistake is to think of God as if he were a human being seeing things unfolding in time. Philosophy tells Boethius that God is timeless, outside time altogether.

What this means is that God grasps everything in an instant. God sees past, present and future as one. We mortals are stuck with one thing happening after another, but that is not how God sees it. The reason why God can know the future without destroying our free will and turning us into some kind of pre-programmed machines with no choice at all is that God observes us at no particular time at all. He sees everything in one go in a timeless sort of way. And, Philosophy tells Boethius, he should not forget that God judges human beings on how they behave, the choices they make, even though he knows in advance what they will do.

If Philosophy is right about this, and if God exists, he knows exactly when I'm going to end this sentence; but it is still my free choice to end with a full stop right here.

You, meanwhile, are still free to decide whether or not to read the next chapter, which looks at two arguments for believing in God's existence.

CHAPTER 8

The Perfect Island
ANSELM AND AQUINAS

We all have an idea of God. We understand what 'God' means, whether or not we believe that God actually exists. No doubt you are thinking about your idea of God now. That seems very different from saying that God actually exists. Anselm (*c.*1033–1109), an Italian priest who later became Archbishop of Canterbury, was unusual in that with his Ontological Argument he claimed to show that, as a matter of logic, the fact that we have an idea of God proves that God actually exists.

Anselm's argument, which he included in his book *Proslogion*, starts from the uncontroversial claim that God is that being 'than which nothing greater can be conceived'. This is just another way of saying God is the greatest being imaginable: greatest in power, in goodness and in knowledge. Nothing greater can be imagined – or that thing would be God. God is the supreme being. This definition of God doesn't seem controversial: Boethius (see Chapter 7) defined God in a similar way, for example. In our minds, we can clearly have an idea of God. That too is uncontroversial. But then Anselm points out that a God that only existed in our minds but not in reality wouldn't be the greatest being conceivable. One that actually existed would certainly be greater. This God *could* conceivably exist – even atheists usually accept that. But an imagined God cannot be greater than an existing one. So, Anselm concluded, God *must* exist. It follows logically from the definition of God. If Anselm is right, we can be certain that God exists simply from the fact that we have an idea of God. This is an a priori argument, one that doesn't rely on any observation about the world to reach its conclusions. It is a logical argument that, from an uncontroversial starting point, seems to prove that God exists.

Anselm used the example of a painter. The painter imagines a scene before painting it. At some stage the painter paints what he imagines. Then the painting exists both in the imagination and in reality. God is different from this sort of case. Anselm believed that it was logically impossible to have an idea of God without God actually existing, whereas we can quite easily imagine the painter who never actually painted the picture he had imagined, so that the painting only existed in his mind, but not in the world. God is the only being like this: we can imagine anything else not existing without contradicting ourselves. If we truly understand what God is we will recognize that it would be impossible for God not to exist.

Most people who have grasped Anselm's 'proof' of God's existence suspect there is something fishy about how he arrives at the conclusion. It just doesn't feel right. Not many people have come to believe in God purely on the basis of it. Anselm, in contrast, quoted from the Psalms that only a fool would deny God's existence. In his own lifetime another monk, Gaunilo of Marmoutiers, however, criticized Anselm's reasoning. He came up with a thought experiment that supported the fool's position.

Imagine that somewhere in the ocean there is an island which no one can reach. This island has incredible wealth, and is filled with all the fruit, exotic trees and plants and animals that are imaginable. It isn't inhabited either, which makes it an even more perfect place. In fact it is the most perfect island anyone can think of. If someone says that this island doesn't exist, there's no difficulty understanding what they mean by this. That makes sense. But suppose they then went on to tell you that this island must really exist because it is more perfect than any other island. You have an idea of the island. But it wouldn't be the most perfect island if it only existed in your mind. So it must exist in reality.

Gaunilo pointed out that if anybody used this argument to try and persuade you that this most perfect island actually existed, you'd probably think it was some kind of joke. You can't conjure a perfect island into real existence in the world just by imagining what it would be like. That would be absurd. Gaunilo's point is that Anselm's argument for the existence of God has the same form as the argument for the existence of the most perfect island. If you don't believe that the most perfect island imaginable must exist, why believe that about the most perfect being imaginable? The same type of argument could be used to imagine all kinds of things into existence: not just the most perfect island, but the most perfect mountain, the most perfect building, the most perfect forest. Gaunilo believed in God, but he thought that Anselm's reasoning about God in this case was weak. Anselm replied, making the point that his argument only worked in the case of God and not with islands, since other things are only the most perfect of their kind, whereas God is the most perfect of everything. That's why God is the only being that *necessarily* exists: the only one that couldn't not exist.

Two hundred years later in a short section in a very long book called *Summa Theologica*, another Italian saint, Thomas Aquinas (1225–74), outlined five arguments, the Five Ways that were meant to demonstrate that God exists. These Five Ways are now much better known than any other part of the book. The second of these was the First Cause Argument, an argument which, like much of Aquinas' philosophy, was based on one that Aristotle had used much earlier. Like Anselm, Aquinas wanted to use reason to provide proof for God's existence. The First Cause Argument takes as its starting point the existence of the cosmos – everything that there is. Look around you. Where did everything come from? The simple answer is that each thing that exists has a cause of some kind that brought it into being and made it as it is. Take a football. That is the product of many causes – of people designing and making it, of the causes that produced the raw materials, and so on. But what caused the raw materials to exist? And what caused those causes? You can go back and trace that. And back and back. But does that chain of causes and effects go on back for ever?

Aquinas was convinced that there couldn't be a never-ending series of effects and their earlier causes going back endlessly in time – an infinite regress. If there had been an infinite regress that would have meant that there would never have been a first cause: something would have caused whatever you think was the first cause of everything, and something must have caused *that* too, and so on to infinity. But Aquinas thinks that logically there must at some point have been something that set everything going in this chain of causes and effects. If he's right about that, there must have been something that wasn't itself caused that began the series of cause and effect which has brought us to where we are now: an uncaused cause. This first cause, he declared, must have been God. God is the uncaused cause of everything that is.

Later philosophers had plenty of responses to this argument. Some pointed out that even if you agree with Aquinas that there must have been some uncaused cause that began everything, there is no particular reason to believe that that uncaused cause was God. An uncaused first cause would have to be extremely powerful, but there is nothing in this argument to suggest that it need have any of the properties religions usually assume God has. For instance, such an uncaused cause wouldn't need to be supremely good; nor would it have to be all-knowing. It could have been some kind of surge of energy rather than a personal God.

Another possible objection to Aquinas' reasoning is that we don't have to accept his assumption that there couldn't be an infinite regress of effects and their causes. How do we know? For every suggested first cause of the cosmos we can always ask 'And what caused that?' Aquinas simply assumed that if we kept asking that question we would come to a point where the answer would be 'Nothing. This is an uncaused cause.' But it is not obvious that this is a better answer than that there is an infinite regress of effects and causes.

The saints Anselm and Aquinas, with their focus on belief in God and their commitment to a religious way of life, provide a stark contrast to Niccolò Machiavelli, a worldly thinker whom some have compared with the devil.

CHAPTER 9

The Fox and the Lion
NICCOLÒ MACHIAVELLI

Imagine you are a prince ruling a city-state such as Florence or Naples in sixteenth-century Italy. You have absolute power. You can issue an order and it will be obeyed. If you want to throw someone into jail because he has spoken out against you, or because you suspect him of plotting to kill you, you can do that. You have troops ready to do whatever you tell them. But you are surrounded by other city-states run by ambitious rulers who would love to conquer your territory. How should you behave? Should you be honest, keep your promises, always act with kindness, think the best of people?

Niccolò Machiavelli (1469–1527) thought that would probably be a bad idea, though you might want to *seem* honest and *seem* good in that sense. According to him, sometimes it is better to tell lies, break your promises and even murder your enemies. A prince needn't worry about keeping his word. As he put it, an effective prince has to 'learn how not to be good'. The most important thing was to stay in power, and just about any way of doing that was acceptable. Not surprisingly, *The Prince*, the book in which he spells all this out, has been notorious ever since it was published in 1532. Some people have described it as evil or at best a handbook for gangsters; others think it the most accurate account ever written of what actually happens in politics. Many politicians today read it, though only some will admit this, perhaps revealing that they are putting its principles into practice.

The Prince wasn't meant to be a guidebook for everyone, only for those who had recently come to power. Machiavelli wrote it while living on a farm about seven miles south of Florence. Sixteenth-century Italy was a dangerous place. Machiavelli had been born and brought up in Florence. As a young man he was appointed as a diplomat, and he had met several kings, an emperor and the Pope in his travels across Europe. He didn't think much of them. The only leader who really impressed him was Cesare Borgia, a ruthless man, the illegitimate son of Pope Alexander VI, who thought nothing of tricking his enemies and murdering them as he took control over a large part of Italy. As far as Machiavelli was concerned, Borgia did everything right, but was defeated by bad luck. He fell ill just at the point when he was attacked. Bad luck played a large part in Machiavelli's life too and it was a topic he thought hard about.

When the immensely rich Medici family, who had previously ruled Florence, returned to power, they threw Machiavelli into prison, claiming that he had been part of a plot to overthrow them. Machiavelli survived torture and was released. Some of his colleagues were executed. But his punishment, because he hadn't confessed to anything, was to be banished. He couldn't return to the city he loved. He was cut off from the world of politics. There, in the country, he would spend his evenings imagining conversations with the great thinkers of the past. In his imagination they discussed with him the best way to keep power as a leader. He probably wrote *The Prince* to impress those in power and as an attempt to get a job as a political advisor. That would have allowed him to return to Florence and the excitement and dangers of real politics. But the plan didn't work. Machiavelli ended up being a writer. As well as *The Prince*, he wrote several other books about politics and was a successful playwright – his play *Mandragola* is still sometimes performed.

So what exactly did Machiavelli advise and why has this so shocked most of his readers? His key idea was that a prince needed to have what he called *virtù*. This is the Italian word for 'manliness' or valour. What does that mean? Machiavelli believed that success depends quite a lot on good luck. Half of what happens to us is down to chance and half is a result of our choices, he thought. But he also believed that you can improve your odds of success by acting bravely and swiftly. Just because luck plays such a large part in our lives, it doesn't mean that we have to behave like victims. A river might flood, and that's something we can't prevent, but if we have built dams and flood defences we stand a better chance of surviving. In other words, a leader who prepares well and seizes the moment when it comes is more likely to do well than one who doesn't.

Machiavelli was determined that his philosophy should be rooted in what really happens. He showed his readers what he meant through a series of examples from recent history, mostly involving people he'd met. When, for example, Cesare Borgia discovered that the Orsini family were planning to overthrow him, Borgia managed to make them feel confident that he knew nothing. He tricked their leaders into coming to talk with him in a place called Sinigaglia. When they arrived, he had them all murdered. Machiavelli approved of this trick. It seemed to him a good example of *virtù*.

Again, when Borgia took control of the region called Romagna he put a particularly cruel commander Remirro de Orco in charge. De Orco terrified the people of Romagna into obeying him. But once Romagna had calmed down, Borgia wanted to distance himself from de Orco's cruelty. So he had him murdered, and left his body cut into two pieces in the city square for everyone to see. Machiavelli approved of this gruesome treatment. It achieved what Borgia wanted, which was to keep the people of Romagna on his side. They were glad that de Orco was dead, but at the same time they realized that Borgia must have ordered his murder and this would have scared them. If Borgia was capable of that sort of violence against his own commander, none of them was safe. So Borgia's action was manly, in Machiavelli's eyes: it displayed *virtù* and was just the sort of thing a sensible prince should do.

This sounds as if Machiavelli approved of murder. He obviously did in some circumstances if the results justified it. But that wasn't the point of the examples. What he was trying to show was that Borgia's behaviour in killing his enemies, and in making an example of his own commander de Orco, worked. It produced the desired effects and prevented further bloodshed. Through his swift, cruel action, Borgia stayed in power and prevented the people of Romagna rising against him. For Machiavelli, this end result was more important than how it was achieved: Borgia was a good prince because he wasn't squeamish about doing what was necessary to keep in power. Machiavelli wouldn't have approved of pointless murder, killing just for the sake of it; but the murders he described weren't like that. Acting with compassion in those circumstances, Machiavelli believed, would have been disastrous: bad both for Borgia, and for the state.

Machiavelli stresses that it's better as a leader to be feared than to be loved. Ideally you would be both loved and feared, but that's hard to achieve. If you rely on your people loving you, then you risk them abandoning you when times get tough. If they fear you, they will be too scared to betray you. This is part of his cynicism, his low view of human nature. He thought that human beings were unreliable, greedy and dishonest. If you are to be a successful ruler, then you need to know this. It's dangerous to trust anyone to keep their promises unless they are terrified of the consequences of not keeping them.

If you can achieve what you are aiming for by showing kindness, keeping your promises, and being loved, then you should do this (or at least appear to do it). But if you can't, then you need to combine these human qualities with animal ones. Other philosophers emphasized that leaders should rely on their humane qualities, but Machiavelli thought that at times the effective leader would have to act like a beast. The animals to learn from were the fox and the lion. The fox is cunning and can spot traps, but the lion is immensely strong and terrifying. It is no good being like the lion all the time, acting simply by brute force, as that will leave you at risk of falling into a trap. Nor can you just be a wily fox: you need the strength of the lion occasionally to keep you safe. But if you rely on your own kindness and sense of justice, you won't last long. Fortunately, people are gullible. They are taken in by appearances. So, as a leader, you may be able to get away with seeming to be honest and kind while breaking your promises and acting cruelly.

Now you've read this, you are probably thinking that Machiavelli was simply an evil man. Many people do believe that, and the adjective 'machiavellian' is widely used as an insult to refer to someone who is prepared to scheme and use people to get their own way. But other philosophers believe Machiavelli expressed something important. Perhaps ordinary good behaviour doesn't work for leaders. It is one thing to be kind in everyday life and to trust people who make promises to you, but if you have to lead a state or a country, trusting other countries to behave well towards you may be a very dangerous policy. In 1938 the British Prime Minister Neville Chamberlain believed Adolf Hitler when he gave his word that he would not try and expand German territory further. That now looks naïve and foolish. Machiavelli would have pointed out to Chamberlain that Hitler had every reason to lie to him and that he shouldn't trust him.

On the other hand, we shouldn't forget that Machiavelli supported acts of extreme brutality against potential enemies. Even in the bloody world of sixteenth-century Italy, his open approval of Cesare Borgia's behaviour seemed shocking. Many of us think there should be strict limits to what a leader can do to his or her worst enemies, and that these limits should be set by law. If limits aren't set, we end up with savage tyrants. Adolf Hitler, Pol Pot, Idi Amin, Saddam Hussein and Robert Mugabe all used the same sorts of techniques as Cesare Borgia to stay in power. Not exactly a good advertisement for Machiavelli's philosophy.

Machiavelli saw himself as a realist, someone who recognized that people are fundamentally selfish. Thomas Hobbes shared that view: it underpins his whole account of how he thought society ought to be structured.

CHAPTER 10

Nasty, Brutish, and Short
THOMAS HOBBES

Thomas Hobbes (1588–1679) was one of England's greatest political thinkers. What's less well known is that he was also an early fitness fanatic. He would go out for a long walk every morning, striding quickly up hills so as to get out of breath. In case he had any good ideas while out he had a special stick made with an inkwell in the handle. This tall, red-faced, cheerful man with a moustache and a little wispy beard had been a sickly child. But as an adult he was extremely healthy and played real tennis into old age. He ate lots of fish, drank very little wine, and used to sing – behind closed doors, and out of earshot – to exercise his lungs. And, of course, like most philosophers, he had a highly active mind. The result was that he lived to 91, an exceptional age for the seventeenth century when average life expectancy was 35.

Despite his genial character, Hobbes, like Machiavelli, had a low view of human beings. We are all basically selfish, driven by fear of death and the hope of personal gain, he believed. All of us seek power over others, whether we realize this or not. If you don't accept Hobbes' picture of humanity, why do you lock the door when you leave your house? Surely it's because you know that there are many people out there who would happily steal everything you own? But, you might argue, only *some* people are that selfish. Hobbes disagreed. He thought that at heart we all are, and that it is only the rule of law and the threat of punishment that keep us in check.

The consequence of this, he argued, was that if society broke down and you had to live in what he called 'a state of nature', without laws or anyone with the power to back them up, you, like everyone else, would steal and murder when necessary. At least, you'd have to do that if you wanted to carry on living. In a world of scarce resources, particularly if you were struggling to find food and water to survive, it could actually be rational to kill other people before they killed you. In Hobbes' memorable description, life outside society would be 'solitary, poor, nasty, brutish, and short'.

Take away the power of the state to prevent people from helping themselves to each other's land and killing whoever they want to, and the result is a never-ending war in which everyone is against everyone else. It is hard to imagine a worse situation. In this lawless world even the strongest wouldn't be safe for long. We all have to sleep; and when we are asleep we are vulnerable to attack. Even the weakest, if cunning enough, would be able to destroy the strongest.

You might imagine that the way to avoid being killed would be to team up with friends. The trouble is you couldn't be sure that anyone was trustworthy. If other people promised to help you, then it might sometimes be in their interest to break their promises. Any activity that required co-operation, like growing food on a large scale, or building, would be impossible without a basic level of trust. You wouldn't know that you'd been tricked until it was too late, and perhaps by that time you'd literally have been stabbed in the back. There would be no one to punish your back-stabber. Your enemies could be everywhere. You'd live your whole life on your own in fear of attack: not an attractive prospect.

The solution, Hobbes argued, was to put some powerful individual or parliament in charge. The individuals in the state of nature would have to enter into a 'social contract', an agreement to give up some of their dangerous freedoms for the sake of safety. Without what he called a 'sovereign', life would be a kind of hell. This sovereign would be given the right to inflict severe punishment on anyone who stepped out of line. He believed that there were certain natural laws that we would recognize as important, such as that we should treat others as we'd expect to be treated ourselves. Laws are no good if there isn't someone or something strong enough to make everyone follow them. Without laws, and without a powerful sovereign, people in the state of nature could expect a violent death. The only consolation was that such a life would be very brief.

Leviathan (1651), Hobbes' most important book, explains in detail the steps needed to move from the nightmarish situation of the state of nature to a secure society in which life is bearable. 'Leviathan' was a gigantic sea monster described in the Bible. For Hobbes it was a reference to the great power of the state. *Leviathan* opens with a picture of a giant towering over a hillside, holding a sword and a sceptre. This figure is made up of lots of smaller people, who are recognizably still individuals. The giant represents the powerful state with a sovereign as its head. Without a sovereign, Hobbes believed, everything would fall apart and society would decompose into separate people ready to tear each other to pieces in order to survive.

Individuals in the state of nature, then, had very good reasons for wanting to work together and seek peace. It was the only way they could be protected. Without that their lives would be terrible. Safety was far more important than freedom. Fear of death would drive people towards forming a society. He thought that they would agree to give up quite a lot of freedom in order to make a social contract with each other, a promise to let a sovereign impose laws on them. They'd be better off with a powerful authority in charge than all fighting each other.

Hobbes had lived through dangerous times, even in the womb. He was born early because his mother had gone into labour when she heard that the Spanish Armada was sailing to England and would probably invade the country. Fortunately it didn't. Later he escaped the dangers of the English Civil War by moving to Paris, but the real fear that England could easily descend into anarchy haunted his later writing. It was in Paris that he wrote *Leviathan*, returning to England soon after it was published in 1651.

Like many thinkers of his day, Hobbes wasn't just a philosopher – he was what we would now call a Renaissance man. He had serious interests in geometry and science, and in ancient history too. As a young man he loved literature and had written and translated it. In philosophy, which he only took up in middle age, he was a materialist, believing that humans were simply physical beings. There is no such thing as the soul: we are simply bodies, which are ultimately complex machines.

Clockwork mechanisms were the most advanced technology in the seventeenth century. Hobbes believed that muscles and organs in the body were the equivalent of these: he frequently wrote about the 'springs' of action and the 'wheels' that move us. He was convinced that all aspects of human existence, including thinking, were physical activities. There was no space for the soul in his philosophy. This is a modern idea that many scientists hold now, but it was radical for his time. He even claimed that God must be a large physical object, though some people took this to be a disguised way of declaring that he was an atheist.

Critics of Hobbes think he went too far in allowing the sovereign, whether it was a king or queen or parliament, to have such power over the individual in society. The state he describes is what we would now call an authoritarian one: one in which the sovereign has almost unlimited power over citizens. Peace may be desirable, and fear of violent death a strong incentive to submit to peace-keeping powers. But to put so much in the hands of an individual or group of individuals can be dangerous. He didn't believe in democracy; he didn't believe in the ability of the people to make decisions for themselves. But if he'd known about the horrors committed by tyrants in the twentieth century, he might have changed his mind.

Hobbes was notorious for refusing to believe in the existence of the soul. René Descartes, his contemporary, in contrast, believed that mind and body were completely distinct from each other. This was probably why Hobbes thought Descartes was much better at geometry than philosophy and should have stuck to that.

CHAPTER 11

Could You Be Dreaming?
René Descartes

You hear the alarm, turn it off, crawl out of bed, get dressed, have breakfast, get ready for the day. But then something unexpected happens: you wake up and realize that it was all just a dream. In your dream you were awake and getting on with life, but in reality you were still curled up under the duvet snoring away. If you've had one of these experiences you'll know what I mean. They're usually called 'false awakenings' and they can be very convincing. The French philosopher René Descartes (1596–1650) had one and it set him thinking. How could he be sure that he wasn't dreaming?

For Descartes philosophy was one among many intellectual interests. He was an outstanding mathematician, perhaps best known now for inventing 'Cartesian co-ordinates' – allegedly after watching a fly walking across the ceiling and wondering how he could describe its position at various points. Science fascinated him too, and he was both an astronomer and a biologist. His reputation as a philosopher rests largely on his *Meditations* and his *Discourse on Method*: books in which he explored the limits of what he could possibly know.

Like most philosophers, Descartes didn't like to believe anything without examining why he believed it; he also liked asking awkward questions, questions which other people didn't get round to asking. Of course Descartes recognized you couldn't go through life constantly questioning everything. It would be extremely difficult to live if you didn't take some things on trust most of the time, as Pyrrho no doubt discovered (see Chapter 3). But Descartes thought it would be worth trying once in his life to work out what – if anything – he could know for certain. To do this he developed a method. This is known as the Method of Cartesian Doubt.

The method is quite straightforward: don't accept anything as true if there is the slightest possibility that it isn't. Think of a big sack of apples. In the sack you know there are some mouldy apples, but you're not sure which ones they are. What you want to end up with is a sack containing just good apples and no mouldy ones. How would you go about achieving that result? One way would be to tip all the apples on to the floor and then look at them one at a time, only putting the ones that you were absolutely sure were good back into the bag. You might throw out a few good apples in the process because they looked as if they might possibly be a bit mouldy inside. But the consequence would be that only good apples would make it into your sack. That's more or less what Descartes' Method of Doubt is. You take a belief, such as 'I am awake reading this now', examine it, and only accept it if you are certain it can't be wrong or misleading. If there is the tiniest room for doubt, reject it. Descartes went through a number of things he believed, and questioned whether or not he was absolutely certain that they were as they seemed to be. Was the world really the way it looked to him? Was he sure he wasn't dreaming?

What Descartes wanted to find was one thing that he could be sure about. That would be enough to give him a foothold on reality. But there was a risk that he might sink into a whirlpool of doubt and end up realizing that nothing at all was certain. He used a kind of sceptical move here, but it differed from the scepticism of Pyrrho and his followers. They were intent on showing that nothing could be known for certain; whereas Descartes wanted to show that some beliefs are immune from even the strongest forms of scepticism.

Descartes sets out in his quest for certainty by thinking first about the evidence that comes through the senses: seeing, touching, smelling, tasting and hearing. Can we trust our senses? Not really, he concluded. The senses sometimes trick us. We make mistakes. Think about what you see. Is your sight reliable about everything? Should you always believe your eyes?

A straight stick put in water seems bent if you look at it from the side. A square tower in the distance might look round. We all occasionally make mistakes about what we see. And, Descartes points out, it would be unwise to trust something that has tricked you in the past. So he rejects the senses as a possible source of certainty. He can never be sure that his senses aren't tricking him. They probably aren't most of the time, but the faint possibility that they might be means he can't completely rely on them. But where does that leave him?

The belief 'I am awake reading this now' probably seems fairly certain to you. You are awake, I hope, and you are reading. How could you possibly doubt it? But we've already mentioned that you can think you are awake in dreams. How do you know you aren't dreaming now? Perhaps you think the experiences you are having are too realistic, too detailed to be dreams; but plenty of people have very realistic dreams. Are you sure you aren't having one now? How do you know that? Perhaps you've just pinched yourself to see if you are asleep. If you haven't, try it. What did that prove? Nothing. You could have dreamt that you pinched yourself. So you *might* be dreaming. I know it doesn't feel like it, and it is very unlikely, but there must be room for a small doubt about whether you are awake or not. So, applying Descartes' Method of Doubt, you have to reject the thought 'I am awake reading this now' as not completely certain.

This shows us that we can't wholly trust our senses. We can't be absolutely sure we're not dreaming. But surely, Descartes says, even in dreams, 2 + 3 = 5. This is where Descartes uses a thought experiment, an imaginary story to make his point. He pushes doubt as far as it will go and comes up with an even tougher test for any belief than the 'Could I be dreaming?' test. He says, imagine there is a demon who is incredibly powerful and clever, but also fiendish. This demon, if it existed, could make it seem that 2 + 3 = 5 every time you did the sum even though it really equals six. You wouldn't know the demon was doing this to you. You'd just be adding numbers up innocently. Everything would seem normal.

There is no easy way of proving that this isn't happening now. Perhaps this fiendishly clever demon is giving me the illusion of sitting at home typing at my laptop, when in fact I'm lying on a beach in the south of France. Or perhaps I'm just a brain in a jar of liquid on a shelf in the evil demon's laboratory. He might have put wires into my brain and be sending electronic messages to me that give me the impression that I'm doing one thing, while I am really doing something completely different. Perhaps the demon is making me think that I'm typing words that make sense, when in fact I am just typing the same letter over and over again. There's no way of knowing. You couldn't prove that that isn't happening, however crazy it might sound.

This evil demon thought experiment is Descartes' way of pushing doubt to its limits. If there was one thing that we could be sure the evil demon couldn't trick us about, that would be amazing. It would also provide a way of answering those people who claim that we can't know anything at all for certain.

The next move he made led to one of the best-known lines in philosophy, though many more people know the quotation than understand what it means. Descartes saw that even if the demon existed and was tricking him, there must be *something* that the demon was tricking. As long as he was having a thought at all, he, Descartes, *must* exist. The demon couldn't make him believe that he existed if he didn't. That's because something that doesn't exist can't have thoughts. 'I think, therefore I am' (*cogito ergo sum* in Latin) was Descartes' conclusion. I'm thinking, so I must exist. Try it for yourself. As long as you have some thought or sensation, it is impossible to doubt that you exist. What you are is another question – you can doubt whether you have a body, or the body that you can see and touch. But you can't doubt that you exist as some kind of thinking thing. That thought would be self-refuting. As soon as you start to doubt your own existence, the act of doubting proves that you exist as a thinking thing.

This may not sound like much, but the certainty of his own existence was very important for Descartes. It showed him that those who doubted everything – the Pyrrhonic Sceptics – were wrong. It was also the start of what is known as Cartesian Dualism. This is the idea that your mind is separate from the body and interacts with it. It is a dualism because there are two types of thing: the mind and the body. A twentieth-century philosopher, Gilbert Ryle, mocked this view as the myth of the ghost in the machine: the body was the machine, and the soul the ghost inhabiting it. Descartes believed that the mind was able to produce effects in the body and vice versa because the two interacted at a certain point in the brain – the pineal gland. But his dualism left him with real problems about how to explain a non-physical thing, the soul or mind, producing changes in a physical one, the body.

Descartes was more certain about the existence of his mind than his body. He could imagine not having a body, but he couldn't imagine not having a mind. If he imagined not having a mind, he'd still be thinking, and so that would prove that he had a mind because he couldn't have thoughts at all if he didn't have a mind. This idea that body and mind can be separated, and that the mind or the spirit is non-physical, not made of blood, flesh and bones, is very common amongst religious people. Many believers hope the mind or spirit will live on after the death of the body.

Proving his own existence, just so long as he was thinking, would not have been enough to refute scepticism, though. Descartes needed further certainties to escape from the whirlpool of doubt that he had conjured up with his philosophical meditations. He argued that a good God must exist. Using a version of St Anselm's Ontological Argument (see Chapter 8), he convinced himself that the idea of God proves God's existence – God wouldn't be perfect unless he was good and existed, just as a triangle wouldn't be a triangle without interior angles adding up to 180 degrees. Another of his arguments, the Trademark Argument, suggested that we know God exists because he has left an idea implanted in our minds – we wouldn't have an idea of God if God didn't exist. Once he was certain that God existed, the constructive phase of Descartes' thought became much easier. A good God wouldn't deceive humanity about the most basic matters. So, Descartes concluded, the world must be more or less as we experience it. When we have clear and distinct perceptions these are reliable. His conclusion: the world exists, and is more or less as it appears, even though we sometimes make mistakes about what we perceive. Some philosophers, however, believe this was wishful thinking, and that his evil demon might just as easily have deceived him about God's existence as about the thought that $2 + 3 = 5$. Without the certainty of a good God's existence, Descartes would not have been able to move beyond his knowledge that he was a thinking thing. Descartes believed that he had shown a way out of complete scepticism; but his critics are still sceptical about this.

Descartes, as we've seen, used the Ontological and Trademark arguments to prove to his satisfaction that God exists. His fellow countryman Blaise Pascal had a very different approach to the question of what we should believe.

CHAPTER 12

Place Your Bets
BLAISE PASCAL

If you toss a coin it can come up heads or tails. There is a 50/50 chance of either, unless the coin has a bias. So it doesn't really matter which side you bet on as it is just as likely each time you toss the coin that heads will come up as tails. If you aren't sure whether or not God exists, what should you do? Is it like tossing a coin? Should you gamble on God not existing, and live your life as you please? Or would it be more rational to act as if God does exist, even if the odds on this being true are very long? Blaise Pascal (1623–62), who did believe in God, thought hard about this question.

Pascal was a devout Catholic. But unlike many Christians today, he had an extremely bleak view of humanity. He was a pessimist. Everywhere he saw evidence of the Fall, the imperfections we have which he thought were due to Adam and Eve betraying God's trust by eating the apple from the Tree of Knowledge. Like Augustine (see Chapter 6), he believed that human beings are driven by sexual desire, are unreliable and easily bored. Everyone is wretched. Everyone is torn between anxiety and despair. We should realize how insignificant we all are. The short time that we are on earth is, in relation to the eternity both before and after our lives, almost meaningless. We each occupy a tiny space in the infinite space of the universe. Yet, at the same time, Pascal believed that humanity has some potential if we don't lose sight of God. We are somewhere between beasts and angels, but probably quite a lot closer to the beasts in most cases and for most of the time.

Pascal's best-known book, his *Pensées* ('Thoughts'), was pieced together from fragments of his writing and published in 1670 after his early death at the age of 39. It is written in a series of beautifully crafted short paragraphs. No one is completely sure how he intended the parts to fit together, but the main point of the book is clear: it is a defence of his version of Christianity. Pascal hadn't finished the book when he died. The order of the parts is based on how he had arranged pieces of paper into bundles tied with string. Each bundle forms a section in the published book.

Pascal was a sickly child, and not physically strong at any time in his life. In painted portraits, he doesn't ever look well. His watery eyes gaze out sadly at you. But he achieved a great deal in a short time. As a young man, encouraged by his father, he became a scientist, working on ideas about vacuums and designing barometers. In 1642 he invented a mechanical calculating machine that could add and subtract by using a stylus to turn dials attached to complicated gears. He made it to help his father with his business calculations. About the size of a shoebox, it was known as the *Pascaline* and although a bit clunky, it worked. The main problem was that it was very expensive to produce.

As well as being a scientist and inventor, Pascal was a superb mathematician. His most original mathematical ideas were about probability. But it is as a religious philosopher and writer that he will be remembered. Not that he would have liked to have been called a philosopher: his writings include many comments about how little philosophers know, and how unimportant their ideas are. He thought of himself as a theologian.

Pascal switched from work in mathematics and science to writing about religion as a young man after he had been converted to a controversial religious sect known as Jansenism. The Jansenists believed in predestination, the idea that we don't have free will, and that only a few people had already been pre-selected by God to go to heaven. They also believed in a very strict way of life. Pascal once scolded his sister when he saw her cuddling her child because he disapproved of displays of emotion. His last years were spent living like a monk, and although in great pain from the illness that eventually killed him, he managed to carry on writing.

René Descartes (the subject of Chapter 11) – like Pascal, a devout Christian, a scientist and a mathematician – believed that you could prove God's existence by logic. Pascal thought otherwise. For him, belief in God was about the heart and faith. He wasn't persuaded by the sorts of reasoning about God's existence that philosophers generally use. He wasn't, for example, convinced that you could see evidence of God's hand in nature. For him, the heart, not the brain, was the organ that leads us to God.

Despite this, in his *Pensées* he came up with a clever argument to persuade those who are unsure whether or not God exists that they should believe in God, an argument that has come to be known as Pascal's Wager. It draws on his interest in probability. If you are a rational gambler, rather than just an addict, you'll want to have the best chance of winning a big prize, but you'll also want to minimize your losses wherever possible. Gamblers calculate odds and, in principle, bet accordingly. So what does that mean when it comes to betting on God's existence?

Assuming you aren't sure whether or not God exists, there are a number of options. You can choose to live your life as if God definitely doesn't exist. If you are right, then you will have lived without any illusion about a possible afterlife, and so you will have avoided agonizing about the possibility that you are too much of a sinner to end up in heaven. You also won't have wasted time in church praying to a non-existent being. But that approach, though it has some obvious benefits, carries with it a huge risk. If you don't believe in God, but God does actually turn out to exist, not only might you lose your chance of bliss in heaven, but you might end up in hell where you will be tortured for the whole of eternity. That is the worst imaginable outcome for anybody.

Alternatively, Pascal suggests, you can choose to live your life as if God does exist. You can say prayers, attend church, read the Bible. If it turns out that God does indeed exist, you win the best possible prize: the serious chance of eternal bliss. If you choose to believe in God, but it turns out that you are wrong, you won't have made a substantial sacrifice (and presumably, you won't be around after your death to learn that you were wrong and feel bad about all that wasted time and effort). As Pascal put it, 'If you win you win everything; if you lose you lose nothing.' He recognized that you might miss out on 'those poisonous pleasures': glory and luxury. But instead you'll be faithful, honest, humble, grateful, generous, a good friend, and will always tell the truth. Not everyone would see it quite in these terms. Pascal was probably so immersed in a religious way of life that he didn't realize that it would be a sacrifice for many non-religious people to devote their lives to religion and live a life of illusion, as they would see it. Nevertheless, as Pascal points out, on one side you have the chance of eternal bliss if you are right, and relatively minor inconveniences and a few illusions if you are wrong. On the other side, you risk the chance of hell, but your possible gains don't compare with an eternity in heaven.

You can't really sit on the fence on the issue of whether or not God exists, either. From Pascal's point of view, if you try to do this it could produce the same outcome for you as believing that God definitely doesn't exist: you could end up in hell, or at least won't get access to heaven. You have to make a decision one way or the other. You really don't know if God exists. What should you do?

Pascal thought it was obvious. If you are a rational gambler and look at the odds with a cool gaze you will see that you should bet on God existing even if, as with tossing the coin, there is only a small chance of being correct. The potential prize is infinite, and the potential loss not great. No rational person would do anything else but gamble on God existing with those odds, he thought. Obviously there is a risk that you bet on God and lose: that God turns out not to exist. But that's a risk you should take.

But what if you see the logic of this, but still don't feel in your heart that God exists? It's really difficult (and perhaps impossible) to talk yourself into believing something which you suspect just isn't true. Try believing there are fairies in your wardrobe. You might be able to imagine that, but that's very different from really thinking there are fairies in there. We believe things that we think are true. That's just the nature of belief. So how does the non-believer who doubts God's existence get to have faith in God?

Pascal had an answer to this problem. Once you've worked out that it is in your best interests to believe in God, then you need to find a way of convincing yourself that God does exist and to have faith. What you should do is imitate people who already believe in God. Spend time in church doing the things that they do there. Take the holy water, have masses said and so on. Very soon you'll end up not just imitating their actions, but actually having the beliefs and feelings they do, he thought. That's your best chance of winning eternal life and avoiding the risk of eternal torture.

Not everyone finds Pascal's argument at all convincing. One of the most obvious problems with it is that God, if he exists, might not look very favourably on people who only believed in him because it was the safest bet. It seems like the wrong sort of reason to believe in God. It's just too self-interested because it is based entirely on you selfishly wanting to save your own soul at all costs. One risk might be that God would make sure that no one who used this gambler's argument ever got into heaven.

Another serious problem with Pascal's Wager is that it doesn't take into account the possibility that in following it you might have opted for the wrong religion, the wrong God. Pascal presents the option as between faith in a Christian God or believing that there is no God. But there are many other religions that promise everlasting bliss to believers. If one of those religions proves to be true, then by opting for following Christianity the individual who follows Pascal's Wager might cut him or herself off from infinite happiness in heaven as surely as the person who rejects all belief in God would have done. Had Pascal thought about this possibility, he might, perhaps, have been even more pessimistic about the human condition than he was.

Pascal believed in the God described in the Bible; Baruch Spinoza had a very different view of the deity, one that led some to suspect he was an atheist in disguise.

CHAPTER 13

The Lens Grinder
BARUCH SPINOZA

Most religions teach that God exists somewhere outside the world, perhaps in heaven. Baruch Spinoza (1632–77) was unusual in thinking that God *is* the world. He wrote about 'God or Nature', to make this point – meaning that the two words refer to the same thing. God and nature are two ways of describing a single thing. God is nature and nature is God. This is a form of pantheism – the belief that God is everything. It was a radical idea that got him into quite a lot of trouble.

Spinoza was born in Amsterdam, the son of Portuguese Jews. Amsterdam was then popular with people fleeing persecution. But even here there were limits to the views you could express. Although brought up in the Jewish religion, Spinoza was excommunicated and cursed by the rabbis in his synagogue in 1656 when he was 24 years old, probably because his views about God were so unorthodox. He left Amsterdam, later settling in

The Hague. From this point he was known as Benedict de Spinoza rather than Baruch, his Jewish name.

Many philosophers have been impressed by geometry. The Ancient Greek Euclid's famous proofs of various geometrical hypotheses moved from a few simple axioms or starting assumptions to conclusions such as that the sum of the interior angles of a triangle are equal to two right angles. What philosophers usually admire in geometry is the way it moves by careful logical steps from agreed starting points to surprising conclusions. If the axioms are true, then the conclusions must be true. This sort of geometrical reasoning inspired both René Descartes and Thomas Hobbes.

Spinoza did not just admire geometry; he wrote philosophy as if it *were* geometry. The 'proofs' in his book *Ethics* look like geometrical proofs and include axioms and definitions. They are supposed to have the same relentless logic as geometry. But instead of dealing with topics like the angles of triangles and the circumferences of circles, they are about God, nature, freedom and emotion. He felt that these subjects could be analysed and reasoned about in just the same way that we can reason about triangles, circles and squares. He even ends sections with 'QED' which is short for *quod erat demonstrandum*, a Latin phrase meaning 'which was to be proved' that appears in geometry textbooks. There is, he believed, an underlying structural logic to the world and our place in it that reason can reveal. Nothing is as it is by chance, there is a purpose and principle to it all. Everything fits together in one huge system and the best way to understand this is by the power of thought. This approach to philosophy, emphasizing reason rather than experiment and observation, is often labelled Rationalism.

Spinoza enjoyed being on his own. It was in solitude that he had the time and peace of mind to follow his studies. It was probably also safer not to be part of a more public institution, given his views about God. For this reason too his most famous book, *Ethics*, was only published after his death. Although his reputation as a highly original thinker spread during his lifetime, he turned down an offer to take up a teaching post at Heidelberg University. He was, though, happy to discuss his ideas with some of the thinkers who came to visit him. The philosopher and mathematician Gottfried Leibniz was one of these.

Spinoza lived very simply, staying in lodgings rather than buying his own house. He didn't need much money and was able to get by on what he earned as a lens grinder together with some small payments from people who admired his philosophical work. The lenses he made were used in scientific instruments such as telescopes and microscopes. This allowed him to remain independent and work from his lodgings. Unfortunately it also probably contributed to his early death from a chest infection at only 44. He would have breathed in the fine glass dust from grinding the lenses and this almost certainly damaged his lungs.

If God is infinite, Spinoza reasoned, it must follow that there cannot be anything that is not God. If you discover something in the universe that is not God, then God can't be infinite, because God could have in principle been that thing as well as everything else. We are all parts of God, but so are stones, ants, blades of grass, and windows. All of it. It all fits together into an incredibly complex whole, but ultimately everything that exists is part of this one thing: God.

Traditional religious believers preached that God loved humanity and responded to personal prayers. This is a form of anthropomorphism – projecting human qualities, such as compassion, on to a non-human being, God. The most extreme form of this is to imagine God as a kindly man with a big beard and a gentle smile. Spinoza's God was nothing like this. He – or perhaps more accurately 'it' – was completely impersonal and did not care about anything or anyone. According to Spinoza, you can and should love God, but don't expect any love back in return. That would be like a nature lover expecting nature to love him back. In fact, the God he describes is so completely indifferent to human beings and what they do that many thought Spinoza didn't believe in God at all and that his pantheism was a cover. They took him to be an atheist and against religion altogether. How could someone who believed that God didn't care about humanity be anything else? From Spinoza's perspective, though, he had an intellectual love of God, a love based on deep understanding achieved by reason. But this was hardly conventional religion. The synagogue had probably been right to excommunicate him.

Spinoza's views on free will were controversial too. He was a determinist. This meant he believed that every human action was the result of earlier causes. A stone thrown into the air, if it could become conscious like a human being, would imagine that it was moving by its own willpower even though it wasn't. What was really moving it along was the force of the throw and the effects of gravity. The stone just felt that it rather than gravity, was controlling where it went. Human beings are the same: we imagine that we are choosing freely what we do and have control over our lives. But that's because we don't usually understand the ways in which our choices and actions have been brought about. In fact free will is an illusion. There is no spontaneous free action at all.

But although he was a determinist, Spinoza did believe that some kind of very limited human freedom was possible and desirable. The worst way to exist was to be in what he called bondage: at the complete mercy of your emotions. When something bad happens, someone is rude to you, for example, and you lose your temper and are filled with hatred, this is a very passive way to exist. You simply react to events. External happenings cause your anger. You are not in control at all. The way to escape this is to gain a better understanding of the causes that shape behaviour – the things that lead you to be angry. For Spinoza, the best that we can achieve is for our emotions to emerge from our own choices rather than external events. Even though these choices can never be fully free, it is better to be active than passive.

Spinoza is typical of a philosopher. He was prepared to be controversial, to put forward ideas that not everyone was ready to hear, and to defend his views with argument. Through his writing he continues to influence those who read his work, even when they disagree strongly with what he wrote. His belief that God is nature didn't catch on at the time, but since his death he has had some very eminent admirers, including the Victorian novelist George Eliot, who made a translation of his *Ethics*, and the twentieth-century physicist Albert Einstein who, though he couldn't bring himself to believe in a personal God, revealed in a letter that he did believe in Spinoza's God.

Spinoza's God, as we have seen, was impersonal and had no human characteristics, so would not punish anyone for their sins. John Locke, born in the same year as Spinoza, took a very different line. His discussion of the nature of the self was partly inspired by his concern about what might happen on the Day of Judgment.

CHAPTER 14

The Prince and the Cobbler
JOHN LOCKE AND THOMAS REID

What were you like as a baby? If you have one, look at a photograph taken at the time. What do you see? Was that really you? You probably look quite different now. Can you remember what it was like being a baby? Most of us can't. We all change over time. We grow, develop, mature, decline, forget things. Most of us get wrinklier, eventually our hair turns white or falls out, we change our views, our friends, our dress sense, our priorities. In what sense, then, will you be the same person as that baby when you are old? This question of what makes someone the same person over time is one that vexed the English philosopher John Locke (1632–1704).

Locke, like many philosophers, had wide interests. He was enthusiastic about the scientific discoveries of his friends Robert Boyle and Isaac Newton, was involved in the politics of his day and also wrote about education. In the aftermath of the English Civil War, he fled to the Netherlands when accused of plotting to murder the newly restored king, Charles II. From there he championed religious toleration, arguing that it was absurd to try to force people to change their religious beliefs through torture. His view that we have a God-given right to life, freedom, happiness and property influenced the founding fathers who wrote the United States Constitution.

We don't have any photographs or drawings of Locke as a baby. But he probably changed quite a lot as he grew older. In midlife he was a gaunt, intense-looking figure with long straggly hair. As a baby, though, he would have been quite different. One of Locke's beliefs was that the mind of a newborn is like a blank slate. We don't know anything when we are born, and all our knowledge comes from our experience in life. As the baby Locke grew into the young philosopher, he acquired all kinds of beliefs and became the person we think of now as John Locke. But in what sense was he the same person as the baby, and in what sense was the middle-aged Locke the same person as the young man?

This sort of problem doesn't just arise for human beings wondering about their relationship to their past. As Locke noticed, it can even be an issue when thinking about socks. If you have a sock with a hole in it and you patch that hole up, and then patch up another hole, eventually you might end up with a sock that consists just of the patches, with none of the original material there at all. Would that still be the same sock? In one sense it is, because there is a continuity of parts from the original to the completely patched up sock. But in another sense it isn't the same sock, because none of the original material is there. Or think of an oak tree. An oak tree grows from an acorn, loses its leaves each year, gets bigger, branches fall off, but still remains the same oak tree. Is the acorn the same plant as the sapling, and the sapling the same plant as the huge oak?

One way of approaching the question about what makes a human being the same person over time would be to point out that we are living things. You are the same individual animal that you were as a baby. Locke used the word 'man' (meaning by that 'man or woman') to refer to the 'human animal'. He thought it was true to say that over a life each of us remains the same 'man' in that sense. There is a continuity of the living human being that develops in the course of its life. But for Locke being the same 'man' was very different from being the same *person*.

According to Locke, I could be the same 'man', but not the same *person* I was previously. How could that be? What makes us the same person over time, Locke claimed, is our consciousness, our awareness of our own selves. What you can't remember isn't part of you as a person. To illustrate this he imagined a prince waking up with a cobbler's memories; and a cobbler with a prince's memories. The prince wakes up as usual in his palace, and to outside appearances is the same person he was when he went to sleep. But because he has the cobbler's memories instead of his own, he feels that he is the cobbler. Locke's point was that the prince is right to feel that he is the cobbler. Bodily continuity doesn't decide the issue. What matters in questions about personal identity is psychological continuity. If you have the prince's memories, then you are the prince. If you have the cobbler's memories, you are the cobbler, even if you have the body of a prince. If the cobbler had committed a crime, it would be the one with the prince's body that we should hold responsible for it.

Of course in ordinary cases memories don't switch like that. Locke was using this thought experiment to make a point. But some people do claim that it is possible that more than one person can inhabit a single body. That is a condition known as multiple personality disorder, where it appears that different personalities are present within a single individual. Locke anticipated this possibility and imagined two completely independent persons living in one body – one present by day, the other only at night. If these two minds have no access to each other, then they are two persons, on Locke's account.

For Locke, questions of personal identity were closely connected with moral responsibility. He believed that God would only punish people for crimes they remembered committing. Someone who no longer remembered doing evil wouldn't be the same person who committed the crime. In everyday life, of course, people lie about what they remember. So if someone claims to have forgotten what they've done, judges are reluctant to let them off. But because God knows everything, he will be able to tell who deserves punishment and who doesn't. A consequence of Locke's view would be that if Nazi-hunters track down an old man who in his youth had been a concentration camp guard, the old man should only be held responsible for what he can remember, and not for any other crimes. God wouldn't punish him for the actions he'd forgotten about, even if ordinary courts wouldn't give him the benefit of the doubt.

Locke's approach to personal identity also gave an answer to a question that vexed some of his contemporaries. They worried about whether you needed the same body to be brought back to life in order to go to heaven. If you did, what would happen if your body had been eaten by a cannibal or a wild animal? How would you get all the body parts back together to be raised from the dead? If the cannibal had eaten you, then bits of you would have become part of him or her. So how could both the cannibal and the cannibal's meal (i.e. you) both be restored as bodies? Locke made clear that what mattered was that you were the same *person* in the afterlife rather than the same body. On his view you could be the same person if you had the same memories, even if these were attached to a different body.

One consequence of Locke's view is that you probably aren't the same person as the baby in the photograph. You are the same individual, but unless you can remember being a baby, you can't be the same person. Your personal identity only extends as far back as your memory. As your memories fade in old age, too, the extent of what you are as a person will also shrink.

Some philosophers feel that Locke went a bit far with his emphasis on self-conscious memory as the basis of personal identity. In the eighteenth century, the Scottish philosopher Thomas Reid came up with an example showing a weakness in Locke's way of thinking about what it is to be a person. An old soldier can remember his bravery in a battle when he was a young officer; and when he was a young officer he could remember that he had been hit when as a boy he'd stolen apples from an orchard. But in his old age, the soldier can no longer remember this event from his childhood. Surely this pattern of overlapping memories would mean that the old soldier was still the same person as the boy? Thomas Reid thought it was obvious that the old soldier was still the same person as the young boy.

But according to Locke's theory the old soldier was the same person as the young brave officer, but wasn't the same person as the young child who was hit (because the old soldier had forgotten about that). Yet, also according to Locke's theory, the young brave officer was the same person as the child (because he *could* remember his orchard escapade). This gives the absurd result that the old soldier is the same person as the young brave officer, and the young brave officer is the same person as the child; but at the same time the old soldier and the child are not the same person. As a matter of logic that doesn't work at all. It is like saying A = B and B = C, but A doesn't equal C. Personal identity, it seems, relies on overlapping memories, not on total recall as Locke had thought.

Locke's impact as a philosopher rests on far more than his discussion of personal identity. In his great work *An Essay Concerning Human Understanding* (1690), he put forward the view that our ideas represent the world to us, but that only some aspects of that world are as they seem. This stimulated George Berkeley to come up with his own imaginative account of reality.

CHAPTER 15

The Elephant in the Room
GEORGE BERKELEY (AND JOHN LOCKE)

Have you ever wondered if the light really does go off when you shut the fridge door and no one can see it? How could you tell? Perhaps you could rig up a remote camera. But then what happens when you turn the camera off? What about a tree falling in a forest where no one can hear it? Does it really make a noise? How do you know your bedroom continues to exist unobserved when you aren't in it? Perhaps it vanishes every time you go out. You could ask someone else to check for you. The difficult question is: does it carry on existing when *nobody* is observing it? It's not clear how you could answer these questions. Most of us think that objects do continue to exist unobserved because that is the simplest explanation. Most of us too believe that the world we observe is out there somewhere: it doesn't just exist in our minds.

Though according to George Berkeley (1685–1753), an Irish philosopher who became Bishop of Cloyne, anything that stops being observed ceases to exist. If no mind is directly aware of the book you are reading, it won't exist any more. When you *are* looking at the book you can see and touch the pages, but all that means for Berkeley is that you have experiences. It doesn't mean that there is something out there in the world causing these experiences. The book is just a collection of ideas in your mind and in other people's minds (and perhaps in God's mind), not something beyond your mind. For Berkeley, the whole notion of an outside world made no sense at all. All of this seems to go against common sense. Surely we are surrounded by objects that continue to exist whether or not anyone is aware of them, aren't we? Berkeley thought not.

Understandably, many people believed he had gone mad when he first started spelling out this theory. In fact it was only after his death that philosophers started taking him seriously and recognized what he was trying to do. When he heard about Berkeley's theory, his contemporary Samuel Johnson kicked a stone hard in the street and declared, 'I refute it thus'. Johnson's point was that he was certain that material things do exist and aren't just composed of ideas – he could feel that stone hard against his toe when he kicked it, so Berkeley must be wrong. But Berkeley was more intelligent than Johnson believed him to be. Feeling the hardness of a stone against your foot wouldn't prove the existence of material objects, only the existence of the *idea* of a hard stone. It's just that for Berkeley what we call a stone is nothing more than the sensations it gives rise to. There is no 'real' physical stone behind it causing the pain in the foot. In fact there is no reality at all beyond the ideas that we have.

Berkeley is sometimes described as an *idealist* and sometimes as an *immaterialist*. He was an idealist because he believed that all that exist are ideas; he was an immaterialist because he denied that material things – physical objects – exist. Like many of the philosophers discussed in this book, he was fascinated by the relationship between appearance and reality. Most philosophers, he believed, were mistaken about what that relationship was. In particular, he argued that John Locke was wrong about how our thoughts relate to the world. It's easiest to understand Berkeley's approach by comparing it with Locke's.

If you look at an elephant, Locke thought, you don't see the elephant itself. What you take to be an elephant is actually a representation; what he called an idea in your mind, something like a picture of an elephant. Locke used the word 'idea' to cover anything we could possibly think about or perceive. If you see a grey elephant, the greyness can't simply be something in the elephant, because it would look a different colour under a different light. The greyness is what Locke called a 'secondary quality'. It is produced by a combination of features of the elephant and features of our sensory apparatus, in this case the eye. The elephant's skin colour, its texture and the smell of its dung are all secondary qualities.

Primary qualities, such as size and shape, according to Locke, are real features of things in the world. Ideas of primary qualities resemble those things. If you see a square object the real object that gives rise to your idea of that object is also square. But if you see a red square, the real object in the world that causes your perception isn't red. Real objects are colourless. Sensations of colour, Locke believed, come from the interaction between the microscopic textures of objects and our visual system.

There's a serious problem here, though. Locke believed that there *is* a world out there, the world that scientists try to describe, but that we only get at it indirectly. He was a realist in that he believed in the existence of a real world. This real world continues to exist even when no one is aware of it. The difficulty for Locke is knowing what that world is like. He thinks that our ideas of primary qualities such as shape and size are good pictures of that reality. But how could he possibly tell? As an empiricist, someone who believes that experience is the source of all our knowledge, he should have had good evidence for the claim that ideas of primary qualities resemble the real world. But his theory doesn't explain how he could ever know what the real world is like since we can't go and check this. How could he be so sure that ideas of primary qualities, such as shape and size, resemble the qualities of the real world out there?

Berkeley claimed to be more consistent. Unlike Locke he thought that we *do* perceive the world directly. That is because the world consists of nothing but ideas. The whole of experience is all that there is. In other words, the world and everything in it only exist in people's minds.

Everything you experience and think about – a chair or a table, the number 3, and so on – for Berkeley only exists in the mind. An object is just a collection of ideas that you and other people have of it. It doesn't have any existence beyond that. Without someone to see or hear them, objects simply stop existing, because objects aren't anything over and above the ideas that people (and God) have of them. Berkeley summed up this strange view in Latin as '*Esse est percipi*' – to be (or exist) is to be perceived.

So the fridge light can't be on, and the tree can't make a noise when there is no mind there to experience them. That might seem the obvious conclusion to draw from Berkeley's immaterialism. But Berkeley didn't think that objects were continually coming into and out of existence. Even he recognized that that would be weird. He believed that God guaranteed the continuing existence of our ideas. God was constantly perceiving things in the world, so they continued to exist.

This was captured in a pair of limericks written in the early twentieth century. Here's the first one, which highlights the strangeness of the idea that a tree would stop existing if no one observed it:

> There once was a man who said 'God
> Must think it exceedingly odd
>   If he finds that this tree
>   Continues to be
> When there's no one about in the Quad.'

(A 'quad' is the name given to the squares of grass in courtyards in Oxford colleges.) This is surely right. The hardest thing to accept about Berkeley's theory is that a tree wouldn't be there if no one was experiencing it. And here is the solution, a message from God:

> Dear Sir, Your astonishment's odd:
> I am always about in the Quad.
>   And that's why the tree
>   Will continue to be,
> Since observed by Yours faithfully, God.

An obvious difficulty for Berkeley, however, is explaining how we can ever be mistaken about anything. If all that we have are ideas, and there is no further world behind them, how do we tell the difference between real objects and optical illusions? His answer was that the difference between experience of what we call reality and experience of an illusion is that when we experience 'reality' our ideas don't contradict each other. For example, if you see an oar in water, it may look bent at the point where it breaks the surface. For a realist such as Locke, the truth is that the oar is really straight – it just looks bent. For Berkeley, we have an idea of a bent oar, but this contradicts the ideas we will have if we reach into the water and touch it. We'll then feel that it is straight.

Berkeley didn't spend every hour of his day defending his immaterialism. There was much more to his life than that. He was a sociable and likeable man, and his friends included the author of *Gulliver's Travels*, Jonathan Swift. In later life Berkeley hatched an ambitious plan to set up a college on the island of Bermuda and managed to raise quite a lot of money to do this. Unfortunately the plan failed, partly because he hadn't realized how far from the mainland Bermuda was and how difficult it was to get supplies there. He did, however, after his death, have a West Coast university named after him – Berkeley in California. That came from a poem he wrote about America which included the line 'Westward the course of empire takes its way', a line that appealed to one of the university's founders.

Perhaps even stranger than Berkeley's immaterialism was his passion in later life for promoting tar water, an American folk medicine made from pine tar and water. This was supposed to cure just about every illness. He even went so far as to write a long poem about how amazing it was. Although tar water was popular for a time, and may even have worked as a cure for minor ailments since it does have mild antiseptic properties, it is, rightly, not a popular cure now. Berkeley's idealism hasn't caught on either.

Berkeley is an example of a philosopher who was prepared to follow an argument wherever it went, even when it seemed to lead to conclusions that defied common sense. Voltaire, in contrast, had little time for this kind of thinker, or, indeed, for most philosophers.

CHAPTER 16

The Best of All Possible Worlds?
VOLTAIRE AND GOTTFRIED LEIBNIZ

If you were designing the world would you have done it this way? Probably not. But in the eighteenth century some people argued that theirs was the best of all possible worlds. 'Whatever is, is right,' declared the English poet Alexander Pope (1688–1744). Everything in the world is the way it is for a reason: it's all God's work and God is good and all-powerful. So even if things seem to be going badly, they're not. Disease, floods, earthquakes, forest fires, drought – they're all just part of God's plan. Our mistake is to focus close up on individual details rather than the larger picture. If we could stand back and see the universe from where God sits we would recognize the perfection of it, how each piece fits together and everything that seems evil is really part of a much larger plan.

Pope was not alone in his optimism. The German philosopher Gottfried Wilhelm Leibniz (1646–1716) used his Principle of Sufficient Reason to come to the same conclusion.

He assumed that there must be a logical explanation for every-thing. Since God is perfect in every respect – that is part of the standard definition of God – it followed from this that God must have had excellent reasons for making the universe in precisely the form that he did. Nothing could have been left to chance. God did not create an absolutely perfect world in every respect – that would have made the world into God, since God is the most perfect thing that there is or can be. But he must have made the best of all possible worlds, the one with the least amount of evil needed to achieve that result. There couldn't have been a better way of putting the bits together than this: no design would have produced more goodness using less evil.

François-Marie Arouet (1694–1778), better known as Voltaire, didn't see it this way. He took no comfort at all from this 'proof' that everything is going well. He was deeply suspicious of philo-sophical systems and the kind of thinkers who believe they have all the answers. This French playwright, satirist, fiction writer and thinker was well known throughout Europe for his outspoken views. The most famous sculpture of him, by Jean-Antoine Houdon, captures the tight-lipped smile and laughter lines of this witty, brave man. A champion of free speech and religious toleration, he was a controversial figure. He is, for instance, supposed to have declared, 'I hate what you say, but will defend to the death your right to say it', a powerful defence of the idea that even views that you despise deserve to be heard. In eighteenth-century Europe, however, the Catholic Church strictly controlled what could be published. Many of Voltaire's plays and books were censored and burned in public and he was even imprisoned in the Bastille in Paris because he had insulted a powerful aristocrat. But none of this stopped him challenging the prejudices and pretensions of those around him. He is best known today, though, as the author of *Candide* (1759).

In this short philosophical novel he completely undermined the kind of optimism about humanity and the universe that Pope and Leibniz had expressed, and he did it in such an entertaining way that the book became an instant bestseller. Wisely Voltaire left his name off the title page, otherwise its publication would have landed him in prison again for making fun of religious beliefs.

Candide is the central character. His name suggests innocence and purity. At the start of the book, he is a young servant who falls hopelessly in love with his master's daughter, Cunégonde, but is chased out of her father's castle when he is caught in a compromising position with her. From then on, in a fast-moving and often fantastical tale, he travels through real and imaginary countries with his philosophy tutor Dr Pangloss, until he finally meets up with his lost love Cunégonde again, though by now she is old and ugly. In a series of comical episodes Candide and Pangloss witness terrible events and encounter a range of characters along the way, all of whom have themselves suffered terrible misfortunes.

Voltaire uses the philosophy tutor, Pangloss, to spout a caricatured version of Leibniz's philosophy, which the writer then pokes fun at. Whatever happens, whether it is a natural disaster, torture, war, rape, religious persecution or slavery, Pangloss treats it as further confirmation that they live in the best of all possible worlds. Rather than causing him to rethink his beliefs, each disaster just increases his confidence that everything is for the best and this is how things had to be to produce the most perfect situation. Voltaire takes great delight in revealing Pangloss' refusal to see what is in front of him, and this is meant to mock Leibniz's optimism. But to be fair to Leibniz, his point wasn't that evil doesn't occur, but rather that the evil that does exist was needed to bring about the best possible world. It does, however, suggest that there is so much evil in the world that it is hardly likely that Leibniz was right – this can't be the minimum needed to achieve a good result. There is just too much pain and suffering in the world for that to be true.

In 1755 one of the worst natural disasters of the eighteenth century occurred: the Lisbon earthquake that killed more than 20,000 people. This Portuguese city was devastated not just by the earthquake, but also by the tsunami that followed, and then by fires that raged for days. The suffering and loss of life shook Voltaire's belief in God. He couldn't understand how an event like this could be part of a larger plan. The scale of suffering didn't make any sense to him. Why would a good God allow this to happen? Nor could he see why Lisbon was the target. Why there and not somewhere else?

In a key episode in *Candide*, Voltaire used this real tragedy to help make his case against the optimists. The travellers are ship-wrecked near Lisbon in a storm that kills almost everyone else on board their ship. The only one of the crew to survive was a sailor who had apparently deliberately drowned one of their friends. But despite the obvious lack of justice in this, Pangloss still sees everything that happens through the filter of his philo-sophical optimism. Arriving in Lisbon just after the earthquake has devastated the city and left tens of thousands dead or dying around him, Pangloss continues, absurdly, to maintain that all is well. In the rest of the book things get even worse for Pangloss – he is hanged, dissected alive, beaten and made to row a galley. But he still clings to his faith that Leibniz was right to believe in a pre-established harmony of everything that is. There is no experience that will budge the stubborn philosophy teacher from his beliefs.

Unlike Pangloss, Candide is gradually changed by what he witnesses. Although at the start of their journey he shares his teacher's views, by the end of the book his experiences have made him sceptical about all philosophy and he opts for a more practical solution to life's problems.

Candide and Cunégonde have been reunited, and they are living together with Pangloss and several of the other characters on a small farm. One character, Martin, suggests that the only way to make life bearable is to stop philosophizing and get down to work. For the first time they start to co-operate and each gets on with what he or she is best at. When Pangloss starts to argue that everything bad that has happened in their lives was a necessary evil that led to this happy conclusion, Candide tells him that's all very well, but 'we must cultivate our garden'. These are the final words of the story, and are intended to convey a strong message to the reader. The phrase is the moral of the book, the punchline of this extended joke. At one level, within the story, Candide is simply saying that they need to get on with the work of farming, they need to keep themselves occupied. At a deeper level, though, cultivating our garden, for Voltaire, is a metaphor for doing something useful for humanity rather than just talking about abstract philosophical questions. That's what the characters in the book need to do to flourish and be happy. But, Voltaire hints strongly, this isn't just what Candide and his friends should do. It's what we all ought to do.

Voltaire was unusual amongst philosophers in being rich. As a young man he had been part of a syndicate that had found a flaw in the state lottery and had bought thousands of winning tickets. He invested wisely and became even richer. This gave him the financial freedom to champion the causes he believed in. Rooting out injustice was his passion. One of his most impressive acts was to defend the reputation of Jean Calas, who had been tortured and executed for supposedly murdering his own son. Calas was clearly innocent: his son had committed suicide, but the court had ignored the evidence. Voltaire managed to get the judgment overturned. There was no chance of consolation for poor Jean Calas, who had protested his innocence to his last breath; but at least his 'accomplices' were freed. This is what 'cultivating our garden' meant in practice for Voltaire.

From the way Voltaire mocks Pangloss' 'proof' that God has produced the best of all possible worlds, you might assume that *Candide*'s author was an atheist. In fact, although he had no time for organized religion, he was a deist, someone who believes that there is visible evidence of God's existence and design to be found in nature. For him, looking up at the night sky was all it took to prove that a Creator exists. David Hume was highly sceptical of this idea. His criticisms of this style of reasoning are devastating.

CHAPTER 17

The Imaginary Watchmaker
David Hume

Take a look in the mirror at one of your eyes. It has a lens that focuses the image, an iris that adapts to changing light, and eyelids and eyelashes to protect it. If you look to one side, the eyeball swivels in its socket. It's also quite beautiful. How did that happen? It's an amazing bit of engineering. How could an eye have turned out this way just by chance?

Imagine stumbling through a jungle on a deserted island, and coming to a clearing. You clamber over the tumbled remains of a palace with walls, stairs, pathways and courtyards. You know it couldn't have got there by chance. Someone must have designed it, some kind of architect. If you find a watch when you are out for a walk it is quite reasonable to assume that it has been made by a watchmaker, and that it was designed for a purpose: to tell the time. Those tiny cogwheels didn't just fall into place by themselves. Someone must have thought it all through. All these examples seem to point to the same thing:

objects that look as if they have been designed almost certainly have been.

Well then, think of nature: trees, flowers, mammals, birds, reptiles, insects, even amoebae. These things also look as if they have been designed. Living organisms are much more complicated than any watch. Mammals have complex nerve systems, blood pumping round their body, and are usually very well suited to the places they inhabit. So surely an incredibly powerful and intelligent Creator must have made them. That Creator – a Divine Watchmaker or Divine Architect – must have been God. Or that's what many people thought in the eighteenth century when David Hume was writing – and some still do today.

This argument for the existence of God is often known as the Design Argument. New discoveries in science in the seventeenth and eighteenth centuries seemed to support it. Microscopes revealed the complexity of tiny pond animals; telescopes showed the beauty and regularity of the solar system and the Milky Way. These too seemed to have been put together with great precision.

The Scottish philosopher David Hume (1711–76) wasn't convinced. Influenced by Locke, he set out to explain the nature of humanity and our place in the universe by considering how we acquire knowledge and the limits of what we can learn by using reason. Like Locke, he believed that our knowledge comes from observation and experience, so he was particularly interested in an argument for God's existence that began with observation of some aspects of the world.

He believed the Design Argument was based on bad logic. His *Enquiry Concerning Human Understanding* (1748) included a chapter attacking the idea that we can prove God's existence in this way. That chapter and one arguing that it was never reasonable to believe eyewitness reports of miracles were extremely controversial. At the time in Britain it was difficult to be openly against religious beliefs. This meant Hume never got a job at a university despite being one of the great thinkers of his time. His friends gave him good advice when they told him not to allow publication of his most powerful attack on the usual arguments for God's existence, his *Dialogues Concerning Natural Religion* (1779), until after his death.

Does the Design Argument prove the existence of God? Hume thought it didn't. The argument does not provide enough evidence to conclude that an all-powerful, all-knowing and all-good being must exist. Most of Hume's philosophy concentrated on the kind of evidence we can give in support of our beliefs. The Design Argument is based on the fact that the world appears to be designed. But, Hume argued, just because it looks designed, it doesn't follow that it really was designed; nor does it follow that God was the designer. How did he arrive at that conclusion?

Imagine an old-fashioned set of weighing scales partly behind a screen. You can only see one of the two pans of the scales. If you see that pan going up, all you can know is that whatever is in the other pan is heavier than the one you can see. You can't tell what colour it is, whether it is cube-shaped or spherical, whether it has words written on it, or is covered in fur, or anything else.

In this example we're thinking about causes and effects. In answer to the question 'What *caused* the pan to move upwards?' all you can answer is, 'The *cause* was something heavier in the other pan.' You see the *effect* – the pan going up – and try to work out the cause from that. But without further evidence there's not a lot more you can say. Anything you do say is pure guesswork and we have no way of telling whether it is true or not if we can't look behind the screen. Hume thought we are in a similar situation with the world around us. We see the effects of various causes, and try to work out the most likely explanation of these effects. We see a human eye, a tree, a mountain, and they might well appear to be designed. But what can we say about their probable designer? The eye looks as if an eye-maker has thought about how best to make it work. It doesn't follow from this, though, that the eye-maker was God. Why not?

God is usually thought of as having the three special powers already mentioned: he is all-powerful, all-knowing and all-good. Even if you reach the conclusion that something very powerful made the human eye, you don't have evidence to say that it was all-powerful. The eye has some flaws. Things go wrong: many people need spectacles to see properly, for example. Would an all-powerful, all-knowing and all-good God have designed the eye just this way? Possibly. But the evidence we get from looking at the eye doesn't *show* this. At best it shows that something highly intelligent and very powerful and skilful made it.

But does it even show that? There are other possible explanations. How do we know the eye wasn't designed by a team of lesser gods all working together? Most complex machinery is put together by a team of people; why doesn't the same hold for eyes and other natural objects, assuming they are put together at all? Most buildings are built by a team of builders; why should an eye be different? Or perhaps the eye was made by a very old god who has since died. Or a very young god who was still learning how to design perfect eyes. Because we don't have evidence to decide between these different stories, we can't be sure just from looking at the eye – an apparently designed object – that it was definitely made by a single living God with the traditional powers. If you start thinking clearly in this area,

Hume believed, you will be very limited in the conclusions you can draw.

Another argument that Hume attacked was the Argument from Miracles. Most religions claim that miracles have happened. People are raised from the dead, walk on water, or make unexpected recoveries from illness; statues talk or cry, the list goes on. But should we believe that miracles have happened just because other people tell us they have? Hume thought not. He was deeply sceptical about that idea. If someone tells you that a man has miraculously recovered from an illness, what does that mean? For something to be a miracle, Hume thought, it had to defy a law of nature. A law of nature was something like 'No one dies and comes back to life again' or 'Statues never talk' or 'No one can walk on water'. There is a huge amount of evidence that these laws of nature hold. But if someone witnesses a miracle, why shouldn't we believe them? Think about what you would say if your friend came running into the room now and told you that she had seen someone walking on water.

Hume's view was that there were always more plausible explanations of what was going on. If your friend tells you that she saw someone walking on water, it is always more likely that she is either deceiving you, or has been mistaken herself, than that she has witnessed a genuine miracle. We know that some people delight in being the centre of attention and are prepared to lie to get there. So that's one possible explanation. But we also know that all of us can get things wrong. We make mistakes all the time about what we see and hear. Often we want to believe that we have seen something unusual and so avoid the more obvious explanation. Even today there are many people who jump to the conclusion that every unexplained sound late at night is the result of supernatural activity – ghosts moving about – rather than being due to more ordinary causes such as mice or the wind.

Although he regularly criticized the arguments used by religious believers, Hume never openly declared that he was an atheist. He may not have been. His published views could be read as claiming that there is a divine intelligence behind everything in the universe, it's just that we can never say much about the qualities of that divine intelligence. Our powers of reason, when used logically, don't tell us much at all about what qualities this 'God' must have. On the basis of this, some philosophers think he was an agnostic. But he probably was an atheist by the end of his life, even if he stopped short of that before then. When his friends came to visit him in Edinburgh in the summer of 1776 as he was dying he made clear that he wasn't about to have a deathbed conversion. Far from it. James Boswell, a Christian, asked him whether he was worried about what would happen after he died. Hume told him he had absolutely no hope that he would survive death. He gave the answer that Epicurus might have given (see Chapter 4): he was, he said, no more worried about the time after his death than he was about the time he had not existed before his birth.

Hume had many brilliant contemporaries, many of whom he knew personally. One of them, Jean-Jacques Rousseau, made a significant impact on political philosophy.

CHAPTER 18

Born Free
JEAN-JACQUES ROUSSEAU

In 1766 a small dark-eyed man in a long fur coat went to see a play at the Drury Lane theatre in London. Most of the people there, including the king, George III, were more interested in this foreign visitor than in the play being performed on stage. *He* seemed uncomfortable and was worried about his Alsatian dog, which he'd had to leave locked in his room. This man didn't enjoy the sort of attention he got in the theatre and would have been far happier out in the country somewhere on his own looking for wild flowers. But who was he? And why did everyone find him so fascinating? The answer is that this was the great Swiss thinker and writer, Jean-Jacques Rousseau (1712–78). A literary and philosophical sensation, Rousseau's arrival in London, at David Hume's invitation, caused the sort of commotion and crowds that a famous pop star would today.

By this time the Catholic Church had banned several of his books because they contained unconventional religious ideas.

Rousseau believed that true religion came from the heart and didn't need religious ceremonies. But it was his political ideas that caused the most trouble.

'Man was born free, and everywhere he is in chains,' he declared at the beginning of his book, *The Social Contract*. It's no surprise that revolutionaries learnt these words by heart. Maximilien Robespierre, like many of the leaders of the French Revolution, found them inspirational. The revolutionaries wanted to break the chains that the rich had placed on so many of the poor. Some of them were starving while their rich masters enjoyed a high life. Like Rousseau, the revolutionaries were angry about how the wealthy behaved while the poor could barely find enough to eat. They wanted true freedom together with equality and brotherhood. It's unlikely, though, that Rousseau, who had died a decade before, would have approved of Robespierre sending his enemies to the guillotine in a 'reign of terror'. Cutting off your opponents' heads was closer in spirit to Machiavelli's thinking than to his.

According to Rousseau, human beings are naturally good. Left to our own devices, living in a forest, we wouldn't cause many problems. But take us out of this state of nature and put us in cities and things start to go wrong. We become obsessed with trying to dominate other people, and with getting other people's attention. This competitive approach to life has terrible psychological effects and the invention of money just makes it all far worse. Envy and greed were the result of living together in cities. In the wild, individual 'noble savages' would be healthy, strong and, above all, free, but civilization seemed to be corrupting human beings, Rousseau felt. Nevertheless, he was optimistic about finding a better way of organizing society, one that would allow individuals to flourish and be fulfilled, yet which would be harmonious with everyone working towards a common good.

The problem he set himself in *The Social Contract* (1762) was to find a way for people to live together that would allow everyone to be as free as they were outside society while still obeying the laws of the state. This sounds impossible to achieve. And perhaps it is. If the cost of becoming part of society was a kind of enslavement, that would be too high a price to pay. Freedom and strict rules imposed by society don't go together, since the rules can be like chains preventing some sorts of action. But Rousseau believed that there was a way out. His solution was based on his idea of the General Will.

The General Will is whatever is best for the whole community, the whole state. When people choose to group together for protection, it seems that they have to give up many of their freedoms. That's what Hobbes and Locke both thought. It's hard to see how you can remain genuinely free and yet live in a large group of people – there have to be laws to keep everyone in check and some restrictions on behaviour. But Rousseau believed that as an individual living within a state you can both be free *and* obey the laws of the state, and that rather than being in opposition, these ideas of freedom and obedience can combine.

It's easy to misunderstand what Rousseau meant by the General Will. Here's a modern example. If you asked most people, they'd prefer not to have to pay high taxes. In fact that is a common way for governments to get elected: they simply promise to lower the rate of taxation. Given the choice between paying 20 per cent of their earnings as tax and 5 per cent of their earnings as tax, most people would prefer to pay the lower amount. But that is not the General Will. What everyone says they want if you ask them is what Rousseau would call the Will of All. In contrast, the General Will is what they *ought* to want, what would be good for the whole community, not just for each person within it thinking selfishly. When working out what the

General Will is we have to ignore self-interest and focus on the good of the whole society, the common good. If we accept that many services, such as the upkeep of roads, need to be paid for from taxation then it is good for the whole community that taxes are high enough to make this possible. If they are too low, then the whole society will suffer. That then is the General Will: that taxes should be high enough to provide a good level of services.

When people get together and form a society, they become a kind of person. Each individual is then part of a greater whole. The way Rousseau felt that they could stay truly free in society was to obey laws that were in line with the General Will. These laws were created by a clever legislator. This person's job was to create a legal system that helped individuals keep in line with the General Will, rather than pursuing selfish interests at others' expense. True freedom, for Rousseau, is being part of a group of people doing what is in the interest of that community. Your wishes should coincide with what is best for all, and laws should help you to avoid acting selfishly.

But what if you oppose what would be best for your city-state? You, as an individual, may not want to conform with the General Will. Rousseau had an answer here. But it's not one that most people would like to hear. He famously, and rather worryingly, declared that if someone failed to recognize that obeying a law was in the interest of the community, then that person should be 'forced to be free'. His point was that anyone who opposed something that was really in the interest of their society, while they might feel they were choosing freely, wouldn't genuinely be free unless they fell into line and conformed with the General Will. How could you *force* someone to be free? If I forced you to read the rest of this book, then that wouldn't be a free choice you had made, would it? Surely forcing someone to do something is the opposite of letting them make a free choice.

For Rousseau, however, this wasn't a contradiction. The person who couldn't identify the right thing to do would become freer by being forced to conform. Since everyone in a society is part of this larger group, we need to recognize that what we should do is follow the General Will, not our selfish individual choices. On this view, only when we follow the General Will are we truly free, even if we are forced to do so. That is Rousseau's belief, but many later thinkers, including John Stuart Mill (see Chapter 24), have argued that political freedom should be freedom for the individual to make his or her own choices as far as possible. Indeed, there is something slightly sinister about the idea of Rousseau, who had complained about humanity being in chains, suggesting that forcing someone to do something is another kind of freedom.

Rousseau spent much of his life travelling from country to country to escape persecution. Immanuel Kant in contrast barely left his home town, though the impact of his thought was felt throughout Europe.

CHAPTER 19

Rose-Tinted Reality
IMMANUEL KANT (1)

If you are wearing rose-tinted spectacles they will colour every aspect of your visual experience. You may forget that you are wearing them, but they will still affect what you see. Immanuel Kant (1724–1804) believed that we are all walking around understanding the world through a filter like this. The filter is the human mind. It determines how we experience everything and imposes a certain shape on that experience. Everything we perceive takes place in time and space, and every change has a cause. But according to Kant, that is not because of the way reality ultimately is: it is a contribution of our minds. We don't have direct access to the way the world is. Nor can we ever take the glasses off and see things as they truly are. We're stuck with this filter and without it we would be completely unable to experience anything. All we can do is recognize that it is there and understand how it affects and colours what we experience.

Kant's own mind was very ordered and logical. So was his life. He never married and he imposed a strict pattern to each day. In order not to waste any time, he had his servant wake him at 5 a.m. He would then drink some tea, smoke a pipe, and begin work. He was extremely productive, writing numerous books and essays. Then he would lecture at the university. In the afternoon, he would go for a walk at 4.30 – exactly the same time each day – up and down his street precisely eight times. In fact people who lived in his home town of Königsberg (now Kaliningrad) used to set their watches by his walk.

Like most philosophers, he spent his time trying to understand our relation to reality. That, in essence, is what metaphysics is about, and Kant was one of the greatest metaphysicians to have lived. His particular interest was in the limits of thought, the limits of what we can know and understand. This was an obsession for him. In his most famous book *The Critique of Pure Reason* (1781), he explored these limits, pushing right to the boundaries of what makes sense. This book is far from an easy read: Kant himself described it as both dry and obscure – and he was right. Very few people would claim to understand it all, and much of the reasoning is complex and jargon-heavy. Reading it can feel like struggling through a dense thicket of words with little sense of where you are going, and few glimpses of daylight. But the core argument is clear enough.

What is reality like? Kant thought that we can't ever have a complete picture of the way things are. We'll never learn anything directly about what he calls the *noumenal* world, whatever it is that lies behind appearances. Although he sometimes uses the word 'noumenon' (singular) and sometimes 'noumena' (plural) he shouldn't have done (a point Hegel made too, see Chapter 22): we can't know whether reality is one thing or many. Strictly speaking, we can't know anything at all about this noumenal world; at least we can't get information about it directly. We *can* know about the *phenomenal* world, though, the world around us, the world we experience through our senses. Look out of the window. What you can see is the phenomenal world – grass, cars, sky, buildings, or whatever. You can't see the noumenal world, only the phenomenal one, but the noumenal world is lurking behind all our experience. It is what exists at a deeper level.

Some aspects of what exists, then, will always be beyond our grasp. Yet we can, by rigorous thought, get a greater understanding than we could get from a purely scientific approach. The main question Kant set himself to answer in *The Critique of Pure Reason* was this: 'How is synthetic a priori knowledge possible?' That question probably doesn't make any sense to you. It will take a little explaining. But the main idea is not as difficult as it first seems. The first word to explain is 'synthetic'. In Kant's philosophical language 'synthetic' is the opposite of 'analytic'. 'Analytic' means true by definition. So, for example, 'all men are male' is true by definition. What this means is that you can know that this sentence is true without making any observations of actual men. You don't need to check that they are all male, as they wouldn't be men if they weren't male. No fieldwork is required to come to this conclusion: you could sit in an armchair and work it out. The word 'men' has the idea of male built into it. It's like the sentence 'All mammals suckle their young.' Again, you don't need to examine any mammals at all to know that they all suckle their young, as that is part of the definition of a mammal. If you found something that seemed to be a mammal, but which didn't suckle its young, you'd know that it couldn't be a mammal. Analytic statements are really just about definitions, so they don't give us any new knowledge. They spell out what we've assumed in the way we've defined a word.

Synthetic knowledge, in contrast, requires experience or observation and it gives us new information, something that isn't simply contained in the meaning of the words or symbols we use. We know, for example, that lemons taste bitter but only through having tasted them (or because someone else tells us about their experience of tasting lemons). It isn't true by definition that lemons taste bitter – that is something that is learnt through experience. Another synthetic statement would be 'All cats have tails.' This is something that you would need to investigate to find out whether or not it was true. You can't tell until you look and see. In fact some cats, Manx cats, don't have tails. And some cats have lost their tails, but are still cats. The question of whether all cats have tails is, then, a matter of fact about the world, not about the definition of 'cat'. It's very different from the statement 'All cats are mammals', which is just a matter of definition and so is an analytic statement.

So where does that leave synthetic a priori knowledge? A priori knowledge, as we have seen, is knowledge that is independent of experience. We know it *prior* to experience, that is, *before* we've had experience of it. In the seventeenth and eighteenth centuries there was a debate about whether or not we know anything at all a priori. Roughly speaking, empiricists (such as Locke) thought we didn't; rationalists (such as Descartes) thought we did. When Locke declared that there were no innate ideas and that a child's mind was a blank slate, he was claiming that there was no a priori knowledge. This makes it sound as if 'a priori' just means the same as 'analytic' (and for some philosophers the terms are interchangeable). But for Kant it doesn't. He thought that knowledge that reveals truth about the world, yet is arrived at independently of experience, is possible. That's why he introduced the special category of synthetic a priori knowledge to describe this. An example of synthetic a priori knowledge, one that Kant himself used, was the mathematical equation 7 + 5 = 12. Although many philosophers have thought that such truths are analytic, a matter of the definition of mathematical symbols, Kant believed that we are able to know a priori that 7 + 5 is equal to 12 (we don't need to check this against objects or observations in the world). Yet at the same time this gives us new knowledge: it is a synthetic statement.

If Kant is right, this is a breakthrough. Before him philosophers investigating the nature of reality treated it simply as something beyond us that causes our experience. Then the difficulty was how we could ever get access to that reality to say anything meaningful about it that was more than just guesswork. His great insight was that we could, by the power of reason, discover features of our own minds that tint all our experience. Sitting in an armchair thinking hard, we could make discoveries about reality that had to be true, yet weren't just true by definition: they could be informative. He believed that by logical argument he had done the equivalent of proving that the world must necessarily appear pink to us. He'd not only proved that we are wearing rose-tinted spectacles, but had also made new discoveries about the various shades of pink that these glasses contribute to all experience.

Having answered to his satisfaction the fundamental issues about our relation to reality, Kant turned his attention to moral philosophy.

CHAPTER 20

What if Everyone Did That?
IMMANUEL KANT (2)

There's a knock at your door. Standing in front of you is a young man who obviously needs help. He's injured and is bleeding. You take him in and help him, make him feel comfortable and safe and phone for an ambulance. This is obviously the right thing to do. But if you help him just because you feel sorry for him, according to Immanuel Kant, that wouldn't be a *moral* action at all. Your sympathy is irrelevant to the morality of your action. That's part of your character, but nothing to do with right and wrong. Morality for Kant wasn't just about *what* you do, but about *why* you do it. Those who do the right thing don't do it simply because of how they feel: the decision has to be based on reason, reason that tells you what your duty is, regardless of how you happen to feel.

Kant thought that emotions shouldn't come into morality. Whether we have them or not is largely a matter of luck. Some people feel compassion and empathy, others don't. Some are mean and find it difficult to feel generous; others get great enjoyment from giving away their money and possessions to help other people. But being good should be something that any reasonable person should be able to achieve through their own choices. For Kant, if you help the young man because you know it is your duty, then that is a moral action. It's the right thing to do because it is what everyone in the same situation should do.

This may sound strange to you. You probably think that someone who felt sorry for the young man and helped him because of that would have acted morally and was perhaps a better person for feeling that emotion. That's what Aristotle would have thought too (see Chapter 2). But Kant was certain. If you do something just because of how you feel that is not a good action at all. Imagine someone who felt disgust when they saw the young man, but still went ahead and helped him out of duty. That person would be more obviously moral in Kant's eyes than someone who acted from compassion. That's because the disgusted person would clearly be acting from a sense of duty because their emotions would be pushing in the completely opposite direction, encouraging them not to help.

Think of the parable of the Good Samaritan. The Good Samaritan helps a man in need he sees lying by the side of the road. Everyone else just passes by. What made the Good Samaritan good? If the Samaritan helped the man in need because he thought it would get him into heaven, in Kant's view that wouldn't have been a moral action at all. It would be treating the man as a way of getting something – a means to an end. If he helped him simply from compassion, as we've seen already, that would be no good in Kant's eyes. But if he helped him because he recognized that it was his duty, and the right thing for anyone in those circumstances to do, then Kant would agree that the Good Samaritan was morally good.

Kant's view of intentions is easier to accept than his view of the emotions. Most of us do judge each other by what each of us is trying to do, rather than just by what we succeed in doing. Think of how you would feel about being accidentally knocked over by a parent rushing to stop his young child from running into the road. Compare that with how you would feel if someone else had deliberately knocked you over for fun. The parent didn't intend to hurt you. The thug did. But, as the next example shows, having good intentions isn't enough to make your action moral.

There's another knock at the door. You answer. It's your best friend who looks pale, worried and out of breath. She tells you someone is chasing her, someone who wants to kill her. He's got a knife. You let her in, and she runs upstairs to hide. Moments later there is yet another knock on the door. This time it is the would-be killer and he has a crazy look in his eyes. He wants to know where your friend is. Is she in the house? Is she hiding in a cupboard? Where is she? In fact she is upstairs. But you tell a lie. You say she has gone to the park. Surely you've done the right thing by sending the would-be killer out to look for her in the wrong place. You've probably saved your friend's life. That must be a moral act, mustn't it?

Not according to Kant. Kant thought that you should never lie – not in any circumstances. Not even to protect your friend from a would-be murderer. It's always morally wrong. No exceptions. No excuses. That's because you couldn't make a general principle that everyone should always lie when it suited them. In this case if you lied and, without you knowing it, your friend *had* gone out to the park, you would have been guilty of helping the murderer. It would have been to some extent your fault that your friend died.

This example is one Kant himself used. It shows how extreme his view was. There were no exceptions to truth-telling or to any moral duty. We all have an *absolute* duty to tell the truth or, as he put it, a Categorical Imperative to do so. An imperative is an order. Categorical imperatives contrast with hypothetical imperatives. Hypothetical imperatives take the form 'If you want *x*, do *y*'. 'If you want to avoid prison, don't steal' is an example of a hypothetical imperative. Categorical imperatives are different. They instruct you. In this case the Categorical Imperative would simply be 'Don't steal!' It is an order telling you what your duty is. Kant thought that morality was a system of categorical imperatives. Your moral duty is your moral duty *whatever the consequences and whatever the circumstances.*

Kant believed that what makes us human is that, unlike other animals, we can think reflectively about our choices. We would be like machines if we couldn't do things on purpose. It almost always makes sense to ask a human being, 'Why did you do that?' We don't just act out of instinct, but on the basis of reasons. Kant's way of putting this is in terms of the 'maxims' we act from. The maxim is just the underlying principle, the answer to the question, 'Why did you do that?' Kant believed that the maxim underlying your action was what really mattered. He argued that you should only act on maxims that were universalizable. For something to be universalizable it has to apply to everyone. This just means that you should only do things that would make sense for anyone in the same situation as you to do. Always ask the question: 'What if everyone did that?' Don't make a special case for yourself. Kant thought what this meant in practice was that you shouldn't use other people but should treat them with respect, recognizing other people's autonomy, their capacity as individuals to make reasoned decisions for themselves. This reverence for the dignity and worth of individual human beings is at the core of modern human rights theory. It is Kant's great contribution to moral philosophy.

This is easier to understand through an example. Imagine you own a shop and you sell fruit. When people buy fruit from you, you are always polite and give them the correct change. Perhaps you do this because you think it is good for business and will make people more likely to come back to spend their money in your shop. If that's the only reason you give them the right change, then that is a way of using them to get what you want. Kant believed that because you couldn't reasonably suggest that everyone treated everyone else in this way, it wasn't a moral form of behaviour. But if you give them the correct change because you recognize that it is your duty not to deceive others, then that is a moral action. That's because it is based on the maxim 'Don't deceive others', a maxim he thinks we can apply to every case. Deceiving people is a way of using them to get what you want. It can't be a moral principle. If everyone deceived everyone else all trust would break down. No one would believe anything anyone ever said.

Take another example Kant used: imagine that you are completely broke. The banks won't lend you money, you don't have anything that you can sell, and if you don't pay your rent you will be out on the street. You come up with a solution. You go to a friend and ask to borrow some money. You promise to pay him back even though you know that you won't be able to do so. This is your last resort, you can't think of any other way of paying your rent. Would that be acceptable? Kant argues that borrowing from a friend without intending to return the money *must* be immoral. Reason can show us this. It would be absurd for everyone to borrow money and promise to pay it back even though they knew they couldn't. That, again, isn't a universalizable maxim. Ask the question, 'What if everyone did that?' If everyone made false promises like this, promises would become completely worthless. If it isn't right for everyone, it can't be right for you. So you shouldn't do it. It would be wrong.

This way of thinking about right and wrong based on cool reasoning rather than emotion is very different from Aristotle's (see Chapter 2). For Aristotle, a truly virtuous person always has the appropriate feelings and does the right thing as a result of that. For Kant, feelings simply cloud the issue, making it more difficult to see that someone is genuinely doing the right thing, rather than just seeming to. Or to put a more positive spin on this: Kant made morality available to every rational person, whether or not they were fortunate enough to have feelings that motivated them to act well.

Kant's moral philosophy stands in stark contrast to that of Jeremy Bentham, the topic of the next chapter. Where Kant argued that some actions are wrong whatever consequences follow from them, Bentham claimed that it was consequences, and only consequences, that mattered.

CHAPTER 21

Practical Bliss
Jeremy Bentham

If you visit University College London you may be surprised to find Jeremy Bentham (1748–1832), or rather what's left of his body, in a glass case. He is sitting looking out at you, with his favourite walking cane that he nicknamed 'Dapple' resting across his knees. His head is made of wax. The real one is mummified and kept in a wooden box, though it used to be on display. Bentham thought that his actual body – he called it an auto-icon – would make a better memorial than a statue. So when he died in 1832 he left instructions about how to deal with his remains. The idea has never really caught on, though Lenin's body was embalmed and put on display in a special mausoleum.

Some of Bentham's other ideas were more practical. Take his design for a circular prison, the Panopticon. He described it as 'a machine for grinding rogues honest'. A watchtower in the middle allows a few guards to keep an eye on a large number of prisoners without them knowing whether or not they're being watched. This design principle is used in some modern prisons and even several libraries. It was one of his many projects for social reform.

But far more important and influential than this was Bentham's theory about how we should live. Known as utilitarianism or the Greatest Happiness Principle, this is the idea that the right thing to do is whatever will produce the most happiness. Although not the first person to suggest this approach to morality (Francis Hutcheson, for instance, had already done so), Bentham was the first to explain in detail how it might be put into practice. He wanted to reform the laws of England so that they were more likely to bring about greater happiness.

But what is happiness? Different people seem to use the word in different ways. Bentham had a straightforward answer to the question. It's all about how you feel. Happiness is pleasure and the absence of pain. More pleasure, or a greater quantity of pleasure than pain, means more happiness. For him, human beings were very simple. Pain and pleasure are the great guides to living that nature has given us. We seek pleasurable experiences and avoid painful ones. Pleasure is the only thing that is good in itself. Everything else we want because we believe it will give us pleasure or help us avoid pain. So if you want an ice cream, that isn't a good thing to have just for its own sake. The point of the ice cream is that it is likely to give you pleasure when you eat it. Similarly you try to avoid burning yourself because that would be painful.

How do you go about measuring happiness? Think about a time when you were really happy. What did it feel like? Could you put a number on your happiness? For instance, was it at a level of seven or eight out of ten? I can remember a trip on a water taxi leaving Venice that felt like a nine-and-a-half or maybe even a ten when the driver accelerated away with the sun setting over the beautiful view, the spray from the lagoon in my face, and my wife and children laughing with excitement. It doesn't seem absurd to be able to give a mark for experiences like this. Bentham certainly believed that pleasure could be quantified and different pleasures compared on the same scale, in the same units.

The Felicific Calculus was the name he gave to his method for calculating happiness. First, work out how much pleasure a particular action will bring about. Take into account how long the pleasure will last, how intense it is, how likely it is that it will give rise to further pleasures. Then subtract any units of pain that might be caused by your action. What you are left with is the happiness value of the action. Bentham called this its 'utility', meaning usefulness, because the more pleasure an action brings about the more useful it is to society. That's why the theory is known as utilitarianism. Compare the utility of an action with the scores for other possible actions and choose the one that brings about most happiness. Simple.

What about the sources of pleasure, though? Surely it's better to get pleasure from something uplifting like reading poetry than from playing a childish game or eating ice cream, isn't it? Not according to Bentham. How the pleasure is produced doesn't matter at all. For him, daydreaming would be as good as seeing a Shakespeare play if they made you equally happy. He used the example of pushpin – a mindless game popular in his day – and poetry. All that counts is the amount of pleasure produced. If the pleasure is the same, the value of the activity is the same: from a utilitarian view, pushpin can be as morally good as reading poetry.

Immanuel Kant, as we saw in Chapter 20, argued that we have duties, such as 'never lie' that apply in all situations. Bentham, however, believed that the rightness or wrongness of what we do comes down to the likely results. These can differ according to circumstances. Lying isn't necessarily always wrong. There might be times when telling a lie is the right thing to do. If, on balance, greater happiness results from telling a lie than not, then that is the morally right action in those circumstances. If a friend asks you whether a new pair of jeans is flattering or not, someone who followed Kant would have to tell the truth even if it wasn't what their friend wanted to hear; a utilitarian would work out whether greater happiness would result from telling a mild lie. If it would, then the lie is the right response.

Utilitarianism was a radical theory to put forward at the end of the eighteenth century. One reason was that in calculating happiness everyone's happiness was equal; in Bentham's words, 'Everybody to count for one, nobody to count for more than one'. No one gets special treatment. The pleasure of an aristocrat counted no more than the pleasure of a poor worker. That was not how society was ordered then. Aristocrats had a very great influence over how land was used, and many even had a hereditary right to sit in the House of Lords and decide on the laws of England. Not surprisingly, some felt uncomfortable with Bentham's stress on equality. Perhaps even more radical for the time was his belief that animals' happiness was relevant. Because they are capable of pleasure and pain, animals were part of his happiness equation. It didn't matter that animals couldn't reason or speak (though it would have done to Kant); those weren't the relevant features for moral inclusion in Bentham's view. What mattered was their capacity for pain and pleasure. This is the basis of many present-day campaigns for animal welfare, such as Peter Singer's (see Chapter 40).

Unfortunately for Bentham, there's a devastating criticism of his general approach with its emphasis on all possible causes of pleasure being treated equally. Robert Nozick (1938–2002) invented this thought experiment. Imagine a virtual reality machine that gives you the illusion of living your life, but removes all the risk of pain and suffering. Once you have been plugged into this machine for a short while, you will forget that you are no longer experiencing reality directly and will be completely taken in by the illusion. This machine generates a whole range of pleasurable experiences for you. It is like a dream generator – it can make you imagine that, for example, you are scoring the winning goal in the World Cup, or having the vacation of your dreams. Whatever will give you the greatest pleasure can be simulated. Now, since this machine would clearly maximize your blissful mental states, you should, on Bentham's analysis, plug into it for the whole of your life. That would be the best way to maximize pleasure and minimize pain. Yet many people, though they might enjoy experimenting with such a machine from time to time, would refuse to plug in for life because there are other things they value more highly than a series of blissful mental states. What this seems to show is that Bentham was wrong to argue that all ways of bringing about the same amount of pleasure are equally valuable, and that not everyone is guided solely by a desire to maximize their pleasure and minimize their pain. This is a theme that was taken up by his exceptional pupil and later critic, John Stuart Mill.

Bentham was immersed in his own age, keen to find solutions to the social problems that surrounded him. Georg Wilhelm Friedrich Hegel claimed to be able to stand back and get an overview of the entire course of human history, a history that was unfolding according to a pattern that only the most impressive intellects could grasp.

CHAPTER 22

The Owl of Minerva
GEORG W.F. HEGEL

'The owl of Minerva flies only at dusk.' This was the view of Georg Wilhelm Friedrich Hegel (1770–1831). But what does it mean? Actually, that question 'What does it mean?' is one that readers of Hegel's works ask themselves a lot. His writing is fiendishly difficult, partly because, like Kant's, it is mostly expressed in very abstract language and often uses terms that he has himself invented. No one, perhaps not even Hegel, has understood all of it. The statement about the owl is one of the easier parts to decipher. This is his way of telling us that wisdom and understanding in the course of human history will only come fully at a late stage, when we're looking back on what has already happened, like someone looking back on the events of a day as night falls.

Minerva was the Roman goddess of wisdom, and she was usually associated with the wise owl. Whether Hegel was wise or foolish is much debated, but he was certainly influential. His view that history would unfold in a particular way inspired Karl Marx (see Chapter 27) and so certainly changed what happened, since Marx's ideas stirred revolutions in Europe in the early twentieth century. But Hegel also irritated many philosophers. Some philosophers even treated his work as an example of the risk of using terms imprecisely. Bertrand Russell (see Chapter 31) came to despise it, and A.J. Ayer (see Chapter 32) declared that most of Hegel's sentences expressed nothing at all. For Ayer, Hegel's writing was no more informative than nonsense verse and considerably less appealing. Others, including Peter Singer (see Chapter 40), have found great depth in his thought, and argue that his writing is difficult because the ideas he is struggling with are so original and hard to grasp.

Hegel was born in Stuttgart, in what is now Germany, in 1770 and grew up in the era of the French Revolution when the monarchy there was overthrown and a new republic established. He called it 'a glorious dawn' and with his fellow students planted a tree to commemorate the events. This time of political instability and radical transformation influenced him for the rest of his life. There was a real sense that fundamental assumptions could be overturned, that what seemed to be fixed for all time needn't be. One insight this led to was the way in which the ideas that we have are directly related to the time we live in and can't be fully understood outside their historical context. Hegel believed that in his own lifetime a crucial stage in history had been reached. On a personal level he progressed from obscurity to fame. He began his working life as a private tutor to a wealthy family before moving on to be a headmaster of a school. Eventually he was made a professor at the university in Berlin. Some of his books were originally lecture notes written up to help his students understand his philosophy. By the time of his death he was the best-known and most admired

philosopher of his time. This is quite amazing, given how difficult his writing can be. But a group of enthusiastic students
dedicated themselves to understanding and discussing what he
taught and bringing out both the political and metaphysical
implications.

Heavily influenced by Immanuel Kant's metaphysics (see
Chapter 19), Hegel came to reject Kant's view that noumenal
reality lies beyond the phenomenal world. Rather than accepting
that *noumena* lie beyond perception causing our experience, he
concluded that the mind shaping reality just *is* reality. There is
nothing beyond it. But this did not mean that reality remained
in a fixed state. For Hegel, everything is in a process of change,
and that change takes the form of a gradual increase in self-
awareness, our state of self-awareness being fixed by the period
in which we live.

Think of the whole of history as a long bit of paper folded up
on itself. We can't really understand what is there until it has all
been unfolded. Nor can we know what is written on the very last
bit of paper until it is opened out. There is an underlying structure to the way it unfolds. For Hegel, reality is constantly
moving towards its goal of understanding itself. History isn't in
any sense random. It's going somewhere. When we look back
over it we will see that it had to unfold like this. This is a strange
idea when you first hear it. I suspect most people reading this
won't share Hegel's view. History for most of us is closer to how
Henry Ford described it: 'just one damned thing after another'.
It is a series of things that happen without any overall plan. We
can study history and discover the probable causes of events
and predict something of what might happen in the future. But
that doesn't mean it has an inevitable pattern in the way Hegel
thought it did. It doesn't mean it's going somewhere. And it
certainly doesn't mean it is gradually becoming aware of itself.

Hegel's study of history wasn't a separate activity from his philosophy, it was part of it: the main part of it. History and philosophy were entwined for him. And everything was driving towards something better. This wasn't an original idea. Religions usually explain history as leading to some end point, such as Christ's Second Coming. Hegel was a Christian, but his account was far from orthodox. For him, the final result wasn't the Second Coming. For Hegel, history has an end target, one that no one had really appreciated before. It's the gradual and inevitable coming to self-awareness of Spirit through the march of reason.

But what is Spirit? And what does it mean for it to become self-aware? The word for Spirit in German is *Geist*. Scholars disagree about its precise meaning; some prefer to translate it as 'Mind'. Hegel seems to mean by it something like the single mind of all humanity. Hegel was an idealist – he thought that this Spirit or Mind was fundamental and finds its expression in the physical world (in contrast, materialists believe that physical matter is basic). Hegel retold the history of the world in terms of gradual increases in individual freedom. We are moving from individual freedom, via freedom for some people but not others, towards a world in which everyone is free in a political state that allows them to contribute to that society.

One way he thought that we make progress in thought is by a clash between an idea and its opposite. Hegel believed that we can move closer to truth by following his dialectical method. First someone puts forward an idea – a thesis. This is then met with its contradiction, a view that challenges the first idea – its antithesis. From this clash of two positions, a more complex third position emerges, which takes account of both – a synthesis of the two. And then, more often than not, this starts the process again. The new synthesis becomes a thesis, and an antithesis is put against it. All this keeps going until full self-understanding by Spirit occurs.

The main thrust of history turns out to be Spirit under-standing its own freedom. Hegel traced this progress from those who lived under tyrannical rulers in Ancient China and India, who did not know that they were free, through to his own time. For these 'Orientals', only the supremely powerful ruler experi-enced freedom. In Hegel's view, the ordinary people had no awareness at all of freedom. The Ancient Persians were little more sophisticated in their appreciation of freedom. They were defeated by the Greeks, and this brought progress. The Greeks and later the Romans were more aware of freedom than those who went before them. Yet they still kept slaves. This showed that they didn't fully appreciate that humanity as a whole should be free, not just the wealthy or the powerful. In a famous passage in his book *The Phenomenology of Spirit* (1807), he discussed the struggle between a master and a slave. The master wants to be recognized as a self-conscious individual and needs the slave in order to achieve this: but without acknowledging that the slave merits recognition too. This unequal relationship leads to a struggle, with one dying. But this is self-defeating. Eventually master and slave come to recognize their need for each other, and the need to respect each other's freedom.

But, Hegel claimed, it was only with Christianity, which trig-gered an awareness of spiritual value, that genuine freedom became possible. In his own time history realized its goal. Spirit became aware of its own freedom and society was as a result ordered by principles of reason. This was very important to him: true freedom only arose from a properly organized society. What worries many readers of Hegel is that in the sort of ideal society imagined by Hegel those who don't fit in with the powerful organizers' view of society will, in the name of freedom, be forced to accept this 'rational' way of living. They will, in Rousseau's paradoxical phrase, be 'forced to be free' (see Chapter 18).

The end result of all history turned out to be Hegel himself coming to an awareness of the structure of reality. He seemed to think he had achieved that in the final pages of one of his books. That was the point at which Spirit first understood itself. Like Plato (see Chapter 1), then, Hegel gave a special position to philosophers. Plato, you'll remember, believed that philosopher-kings should rule his ideal republic. Hegel, in contrast, thought philosophers could achieve a particular kind of self-understanding that was also an understanding of reality and of all history, another way of enacting the words engraved at the Temple of Apollo in Delphi: 'Know Thyself'. It is philosophers, he believed, who come to realize the ultimate unfolding pattern of human events. They appreciate the way that the dialectic has produced a gradual awakening. Suddenly everything becomes clear to them and the point of the whole of human history becomes obvious. Spirit enters a new phase of self-understanding. That's the theory anyway.

Hegel had many admirers, but Arthur Schopenhauer was not one of them. He thought Hegel wasn't really a philosopher at all because he lacked seriousness and honesty in the way he approached the subject. As far as Schopenhauer was concerned, Hegel's philosophy was nonsense. Hegel, for his part, described Schopenhauer as 'loathsome and ignorant'.

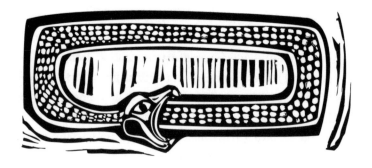

CHAPTER 23

Glimpses of Reality
ARTHUR SCHOPENHAUER

Life is painful and it would be better not to have been born. Few people have such a pessimistic outlook, but Arthur Schopenhauer (1788–1860) did. According to him, we are all caught up in a hopeless cycle of wanting things, getting them, and then wanting more things. It doesn't stop until we die. Whenever we seem to get what we want, we start wanting something else. You might think you would be content if you were a millionaire, but you wouldn't be for long. You'd want something you hadn't got. Human beings are like that. We're never satisfied, never stop craving for more than we have. It's all very depressing.

But Schopenhauer's philosophy isn't quite as dark as this sounds. He thought that if we could only recognize the true nature of reality, we would behave very differently and might avoid some of the bleaker features of the human condition. His message was very close to the Buddha's. The Buddha taught that all life involves suffering but that at a deep level there is no such thing as 'the self': if we recognize that, we can achieve enlight-enment. This similarity was no coincidence. Unlike most Western philosophers, Schopenhauer had read widely in Eastern philosophy. He even had a statue of the Buddha on his desk, next to one of his other great influences, Immanuel Kant.

Unlike the Buddha and Kant, Schopenhauer was a gloomy, difficult, vain man. When he got a job as a lecturer in Berlin, he was so convinced of his own genius that he insisted that his lectures should take place at exactly the same time as Hegel's. This wasn't his greatest idea, as Hegel was very popular with students. Hardly anyone showed up to Schopenhauer's lectures; Hegel's, meanwhile, were packed. Schopenhauer later left the university and lived for the rest of his life on inherited money.

His most important book, *The World as Will and Representation*, was first published in 1818, but he kept working on it for years, producing a much longer version in 1844. The main idea at the heart of it is quite simple. Reality has two aspects. It exists both as Will and as Representation. Will is the blind driving force that is found in absolutely everything that exists. It is the energy that makes plants and animals grow, but it is also the force that causes magnets to point north, and crystals to grow in chemical compounds. It is present in every part of nature. The other aspect, the World as Representation, is the world as we experience it.

The World as Representation is our construction of reality in our minds. It is what Kant called the *phenomenal* world. Look around you now. Perhaps you can see trees, people or cars through a window, or this book in front of you; perhaps you can hear birds or traffic or noises in another room. What you are experiencing through your senses is the World as Representation. That is your way of making sense of everything and it requires your consciousness. Your mind organizes your experience to make sense of it all. This World as Representation is the world we live in. But, like Kant, Schopenhauer believed that there was a deeper reality that exists beyond your experiences too, beyond the world of appearances. Kant called that the noumenal world, and he thought we had no direct access to it. For Schopenhauer, the World as Will was a bit like Kant's noumenal world, though there were important differences.

Kant wrote about *noumena*, the plural of *noumenon*. He thought that reality could have more than one part. It is not clear how Kant knew this, given that he had declared that the noumenal world was inaccessible to us. Schopenhauer in contrast held that we couldn't assume that the noumenal reality was divided at all, since that kind of division requires space and time, which Kant believed were contributed by the individual mind rather than existing in reality itself. Instead Schopenhauer described the World as Will as a single, unified, directionless force behind everything that is. We can glimpse this World as Will through our own actions and also through our experience of art.

Stop reading this and put your hand on your head. What happened? Someone watching you would just see your hand going up and resting on your head. You can see that too if you look in the mirror. This is a description of the phenomenal world, the World as Representation. According to Schopenhauer, though, there is an inner aspect to our experience of moving our body, something that we can feel in a different way from our experience of the phenomenal world in general. We don't experience the World as Will directly, but we do come very close to that when we perform deliberate actions, when we *will* bodily actions, make them happen. That's why he chose the word 'Will' to describe reality, even though it is only in the human situation that this energy has any connection whatsoever with doing something deliberately – plants don't grow deliberately, nor do chemical reactions happen deliberately. So it's important to realize that the word 'Will' is different from ordinary uses of the term.

When someone 'wills' something they have an aim in mind: they're trying to do something. But that is not at all what Schopenhauer means when he describes reality at the level of the World as Will. The Will (with a capital W) is aimless, or, as he sometimes puts it, 'blind'. It isn't attempting to bring about any particular result. It doesn't have any point or goal. It is just this great surge of energy that is in every natural phenomenon as well as in our conscious acts of willing things. For Schopenhauer there is no God to give it direction. Nor is the Will itself God. The human situation is that we, like all reality, are part of this meaningless force.

Yet there are some experiences that can make life bearable. These come mostly from art. Art provides a still point so that, for a short time, we can escape the endless cycle of striving and desire. Music is the best art form for this. According to Schopenhauer that's because music is a copy of the Will itself. This, he felt, explained music's power to move us so profoundly. If you listen to a Beethoven symphony in the right frame of mind you aren't just being stimulated emotionally: you are glimpsing reality as it truly is.

No other philosopher has given such a central place to the arts, so it is not surprising that Schopenhauer is popular with creative people of various kinds. Composers and musicians love him because he believed that music was the most important of all the arts. His ideas have also appealed to novelists including Leo Tolstoy, Marcel Proust, Thomas Mann and Thomas Hardy. Dylan Thomas even wrote a poem 'The force that through the green fuse drives the flower' which was inspired by Schopenhauer's description of the World as Will.

Schopenhauer didn't just describe reality and our relation to it. He also had views about how we should live. Once you realize that we are all part of one energy force, and that individual people exist only at the level of the World as Representation, this should change what you do. For Schopenhauer, harming other people is a kind of self-injury. This is the foundation of all morality. If I kill you, I destroy a part of the life force that joins us all together. When someone harms another person it is like a snake biting its tail without knowing that it is sinking its fangs into its own flesh. So the basic morality that Schopenhauer taught was one of compassion. Properly understood, other people aren't external to me. I care what happens to you because in a way you are part of what we are all part of: the World as Will.

That's Schopenhauer's official moral position. It is questionable, though, whether he achieved anything like this degree of concern for other people himself. On one occasion, an old woman chatting outside his door made him so angry that he pushed her down the stairs. She was injured, and a court ordered Schopenhauer to pay compensation to her for the rest of her life. When she died some years later, Schopenhauer showed no compassion: instead he scribbled the joke-rhyme 'obit anus, abit onus' (Latin for 'the old woman dies, the burden goes') on her death certificate.

There is another, more extreme method for coming to terms with the cycle of desire. To avoid getting caught up in all this, simply turn away from the world altogether and become an ascetic: live a life of sexual chastity and poverty. This, he felt, would be the ideal way to cope with existence. It is the solution many Eastern religions opt for. Schopenhauer, however, never became an ascetic, despite withdrawing from social life as he grew older. For most of his life he enjoyed company, had affairs, ate well. It is tempting to say that he was a hypocrite. Indeed, the vein of pessimism that runs through his writing is so deep in places that some readers thought that if he had been sincere he would have killed himself.

The great Victorian philosopher John Stuart Mill, in contrast, was an optimist. He argued that rigorous thought and discussion could spur social change and bring about a better world, a world in which more people could lead happy and fulfilled lives.

CHAPTER 24

Space to Grow
John Stuart Mill

Imagine that you had been kept away from other children for most of your childhood. Instead of spending time playing, you would have been learning Greek and algebra, taught by a private tutor, or you'd be in conversation with highly intelligent adults. How would you have turned out?

This is more or less what happened to John Stuart Mill (1806–73). He was an educational experiment. His father, James Mill, a friend of Jeremy Bentham, shared John Locke's view that a young child's mind was empty, like a blank slate. James Mill was convinced that if you brought a child up in the right way, there was a good chance that he or she would develop into a genius. So James taught his son John at home, making sure that he didn't waste any time playing with children his own age or learning bad habits from them. But this wasn't simply cramming, forced memorization, or anything like that. James taught using Socrates' method of cross-questioning, encouraging his son to explore the ideas he was learning rather than just parrot them.

The stunning result was that by the age of three John was studying Ancient Greek. By six he had written a history of Rome, and aged seven he could understand Plato's dialogues in the original language. At eight he started to learn Latin. By 12 he had a thorough appreciation of history, economics and politics, could solve complex mathematical equations and had a passionate and sophisticated interest in science. He was a prodigy. In his twenties he was already one of the most brilliant thinkers of his age, though he never really got over his strange childhood and remained lonely and a bit distant throughout his life.

Nevertheless, he *had* turned into a kind of genius. So his father's experiment had worked. He became a campaigner against injustice, an early feminist (he was arrested for promoting birth control), a politician, a journalist, and a great philosopher, perhaps the greatest philosopher of the nineteenth century.

Mill had been brought up as a utilitarian, and Bentham's influence was immense. The Mills would stay at Bentham's house in the Surrey countryside each summer. But, although Mill agreed with Bentham that the right action is always the one that produces the most happiness, he came to believe that his teacher's account of happiness as pleasure was too crude. So the younger man developed his own version of the theory, one that distinguished between higher and lower pleasures.

Given the choice, would it be better to be a contented pig rolling about in a muddy sty and chomping through the food in its trough, or a sad human being? Mill thought it was obvious that we would choose to be a sad human rather than a happy pig. But that goes against what Bentham thought. Bentham, you will remember, says that all that counts are pleasurable experiences, no matter how they are produced. Mill disagreed. He thought that you could have different kinds of pleasure and that some were much better than others, so much better that no quantity of the lower pleasure could ever match the smallest quantity of the higher one. Lower pleasures, such as those an animal can experience, would never challenge the higher, intellectual pleasures, like the pleasure of reading a book or listening to a concert. Mill went further, and said that it would be better to be a dissatisfied Socrates than a satisfied fool. That's because the philosopher Socrates was capable of gaining so much more subtle pleasures from his thinking than the fool could ever achieve.

Why believe Mill? His answer was that anyone who has experienced both higher and lower pleasures prefers the higher ones. The pig can't read or listen to classical music, so its opinion on this wouldn't count. If a pig could read it would prefer reading to rolling in mud.

That's what Mill thought. But some people have pointed out that he assumed that everyone was like him in preferring reading to rolling in the mud. Worse still, as soon as Mill introduces different qualities of happiness (higher and lower) as well as different quantities, it becomes much harder to see how you could ever calculate what to do. One of the great virtues of Bentham's approach was its simplicity, with every kind of pleasure and pain measured in the same currency. Mill gives no way of working out an exchange rate between the different currencies of higher and lower pleasures.

Mill applied his utilitarian thinking to all aspects of life. He thought that human beings are a bit like trees. If you don't give a tree enough space to develop, it will be twisted and weak. But in the right position it can fulfil its potential and reach a great height and spread. Similarly, in the right circumstances, human beings flourish, and that produces good consequences not just for the individual concerned, but for the whole of society – it maximizes happiness. In 1859 he published a short but inspiring book defending his view that giving each person space to develop as they saw fit was the best way to organize society. That book is called *On Liberty* and it is still widely read today.

Paternalism, from the Latin *pater* meaning father, is forcing someone to do something for their own good (though it could equally have been maternalism from *mater*, the Latin for mother). If as a child you were made to eat your greens then you will understand this concept very well. Eating green vegetables doesn't do anyone else any good, but your parents still make you do it for your own good. Mill thought paternalism was fine when it was directed at children: children need to be protected from themselves and have their behaviour controlled in various ways. But paternalism towards adults in a civilized society was unacceptable. The only justification for it was when an adult risked harming someone else by their actions or if they had severe psychiatric problems.

Mill's message was simple. It is known as the Harm Principle. Every adult should be free to live as he or she pleases as long as no one else is harmed in the process. This was a challenging idea in Victorian England when many people assumed that part of the role of government was to impose good moral values on the people. Mill disagreed. He thought that greater happiness would come from individuals having greater freedom in how they behaved. And it was not just government telling people what to do that worried Mill. He hated what he called 'the tyranny of the majority', the way that social pressures worked to prevent many people from doing what they wanted to do or become.

Others may think they know what will make you happy. But they are usually wrong. You know much better than they do what you really want to do with your life. And even if you don't, Mill argued, it is better to let each of us make our own mistakes than to force us to conform with one way of living. This is consistent with his utilitarianism since he believed that increasing individual freedom produces more happiness overall than restricting it does.

According to Mill (who was one himself), geniuses, even more than the rest of us, need freedom in order to develop. They rarely fit into society's expectations about how they should behave and often seem eccentric. If you cramp their development, then we all lose out because they probably won't make the contributions to society that they might otherwise have done. So, if you want to achieve the greatest possible amount of happiness, let people get on with their lives without interfering with them; unless, of course, they risk harming other people by their actions. If you find what they are doing offensive that is not a good reason for preventing them from living this way. Mill was very clear on this point: offence should not be confused with harm.

Mill's approach has some quite disturbing consequences. Imagine a man with no family who decides that he will drink two bottles of vodka every night. It is very easy to see that he is drinking himself to death. Should the law intervene to stop him? No, says Mill, not unless he risks harming someone else. You can argue with him, tell him he is destroying himself. But no one should force him to change his ways; nor should government prevent him drinking his life away. That's his free choice. It wouldn't be his free choice if he was looking after a young child, but as he has no one depending on him, he can do what he likes.

As well as freedom in how to live, Mill thought it was vital that everyone was given freedom to think and speak as they liked. Open discussion was of great benefit to society, he felt, because it forced people to think hard about what they believed. If you don't have your views challenged by people with opposing views, then you will probably end up holding them as 'dead dogmas', prejudices that you can't really defend. He argued for free speech up to the point at which it incited violence. A journalist, he believed, should be free to write an editorial in which he declared that 'corn-dealers are starvers of the poor', but if he waved a placard with the same words on it while standing on the steps of a corn-dealer's house in front of an angry mob, that would be an incitement to violence and so forbidden by Mill's Harm Principle.

Many people disagreed with Mill. Some thought his approach to freedom was too centred on the idea that what matters is how individuals feel about their lives (it is much more individualistic, for example, than Rousseau's concept of freedom, see Chapter 18). Others saw him as opening the doors to a permissive society that would wreck morality for ever. James Fitzjames Stephen, one of his contemporaries, argued that most people should be forced down a narrow channel and not given too many choices about how they live, because so many, given free rein, would end up making bad and self-destructive decisions for themselves.

One area in which Mill was particularly radical at the time he wrote was in his feminism. In England in the nineteenth century married women were not allowed to own property, and had little legal protection against violence and rape by their husbands. Mill argued in *The Subjection of Women* (1869) that the sexes should be treated equally both in law and in society more generally. Some around him claimed that women were naturally inferior to men. He asked how they could possibly know this when women had so often been prevented from reaching their full potential: they were kept away from higher education and many professions. Above all, he wanted greater equality of the sexes. Marriage should be a friendship between equals, he argued. His own marriage to the widow Harriet Taylor, which came very late in their lives, was like this and it brought both great happiness. They had been intimate friends (and perhaps even lovers) while her first husband was alive, but Mill had had to wait until 1851 to become her second. She helped him write both *On Liberty* and *The Subjection of Women*, though, sadly, she died before either was published.

On Liberty was first published in 1859. In the same year another even more important book appeared: Charles Darwin's *On the Origin of Species*.

CHAPTER 25

Unintelligent Design
CHARLES DARWIN

'Are you related to monkeys on your grandmother's or your grandfather's side?' This was Bishop Samuel Wilberforce's cheeky question in a famous debate with Thomas Henry Huxley in Oxford's Museum of Natural History in 1860. Huxley was defending the views of Charles Darwin (1809–82). Wilberforce's question was meant to be both an insult and a joke. But it back-fired. Huxley muttered under his breath, 'Thank you God for delivering him into my hands', and replied that he would rather be related to an ape than to a human being who held back debate by making fun of scientific ideas. He might just as well have explained that he was descended from monkey-like ancestors on both sides – not very recently, but some time in the past. That's what Darwin claimed. Everyone has them in their family tree.

This view caused a great stir almost from the moment his book *On the Origin of Species* was published in 1859. After that it was no longer possible to think of human beings as completely different from the rest of the animal kingdom. Human beings weren't special any more: they were just part of nature like any other animal. This might not come as a surprise to you, but it did to most Victorians.

You might think that all it would take to recognize our closeness to apes would be a few minutes spent in the company of a chimpanzee or gorilla or perhaps even a hard look in the mirror. But in Darwin's day more or less everyone assumed that human beings were very different from any other animal and the idea that we shared distant relatives with them was ridiculous. There were plenty of people who thought that Darwin's ideas were crazy and the work of the devil. Some Christians clung to their belief that the Book of Genesis gave the true story of how God created all the animals and plants in six busy days. God had designed the world and everything in it, each with its proper place for all time. These Christians believed that every species of animal and plant had remained the same since the Creation. Even today some people still refuse to believe that evolution is the process by which we came to be what we are.

Darwin was a biologist and a geologist, not a philosopher. So you might wonder why there is a chapter about him in this book. The reason it's here is that his theory of evolution by natural selection and its modern versions have had a profound impact on how philosophers – as well as scientists – think about humanity. It is the most influential scientific theory of all time. The contemporary philosopher Daniel Dennett has called it 'the single best idea anyone has ever had'. The theory explains how human beings and the plants and animals around them have come to be as they are and how they are all still changing.

One result of this scientific theory was that it became easier than ever before to believe that there is no God. The zoologist

Richard Dawkins has written, 'I can't imagine being an atheist at any time before 1859, when Darwin's *On the Origin of Species* was published.' There were atheists, of course, before 1859 – David Hume, the subject of Chapter 17, was probably one – but there were many more afterwards. You don't have to be an atheist to believe that evolution is true: many religious believers are Darwinists. But they can't be Darwinists *and* believe that God created all species exactly as they are today.

As a young man, Darwin went on a five-year voyage on HMS *Beagle,* visiting South America, Africa and Australia. This was the adventure of his lifetime – as it would be for anyone. Before that he hadn't been a particularly promising student, and no one would have expected him to make such an impressive contribution to human thought. He was no genius at school. His father was convinced that he was going to be a waster, and a disgrace to his family because he spent so much of his time hunting and shooting rats. As a young man he'd started training as a doctor in Edinburgh, but when that didn't work out, he switched to studying divinity at Cambridge University, intending to become a vicar. In his spare time he was an enthusiastic naturalist, collecting plants and insects, but there were no signs that he was going to be the greatest biologist in history. In many ways he seemed a bit lost. He didn't really know what he wanted to do. But the voyage of the *Beagle* transformed him.

The trip was a scientific expedition around the world, partly to map the coastlines of the places the ship visited. Despite his lack of qualifications, Darwin took on the role of official botanist, but he also made detailed observations of rocks, fossils and animals wherever they landed. The small ship quickly filled up with the samples he collected. Luckily he was able to send most of this collection back to England where it was stored ready for investigation.

By far the most valuable part of the voyage turned out to be the visit to the Galapagos Islands, a group of volcanic islands in the Pacific Ocean roughly 500 miles from South America. The *Beagle* reached the Galapagos Islands in 1835. There were plenty of interesting animals to examine there, including giant tortoises and sea-loving iguanas. Though it wasn't obvious to him at the time, the most important for Darwin's theory of evolution were a range of rather drab-looking finches. He shot a number of these small birds and sent them home for further examination. Close study later revealed that there were thirteen distinct species. The small differences between them were mostly in their beaks.

After his return, Darwin abandoned his plans of becoming a vicar. While he'd been travelling the fossils, plants and dead animals he'd sent back had made him quite famous in the scientific world. He became a full-time naturalist and spent many years working on his theory of evolution as well as becoming a world expert on barnacles, those small limpet-like animals that cling to rocks and the hulls of ships. The more he thought about it, the more he was convinced that species evolved through a natural process and were constantly changing rather than fixed for all time. Eventually he came up with the suggestion that plants and animals that were well suited to their environment were more likely to survive long enough to pass on some of their characteristics to their young. Over long periods this pattern produced plants and animals that seemed to have been designed to live in the environments in which they were found. The Galapagos Islands provided some of the best evidence of evolution in action. For example, at some point in history, he thought, finches had found their way there from the mainland, perhaps carried by strong winds. Through many thousands of generations, the birds on each island had then gradually adapted to where they were living.

Not all birds of the same species are identical. There's usually quite a lot of variety. One bird might have a slightly more pointed beak than another, for instance. If having this kind of beak helped the bird survive longer, it would be more likely to breed. For example, a bird that has a beak that is good for eating seeds would do well on an island where there were many seeds around, but probably not so well on an island where the main source of food is from nuts that needed to be cracked. A bird that had a harder time finding food because of its beak shape would find it difficult to survive long enough to mate and produce offspring. That made it less likely that that type of beak would be passed on. Birds with beaks that suited the available food supplies would be more likely to pass that feature on to their offspring. So on a seed-rich island, the birds with good beaks for eating seeds came to dominate. Over many thousands of years this led to a new species evolving, one that was very different from the original type that landed on the island. Birds with the wrong types of beak would have gradually died out. On an island with different conditions a slightly different sort of finch would evolve. Over long periods of time the birds' beaks became better and better adapted to their environment. The varying environments on different islands meant that the birds that thrived were the ones best suited to that place.

Other people before Darwin, including his grandfather Erasmus Darwin, had suggested that animals and plants had evolved. What Charles Darwin added was the theory of adaptation by natural selection, the process that leads the best-adapted to survive to pass on their characteristics.

This struggle for survival explains everything. It isn't just a struggle between members of different species; members of the same species struggle against each other too. They are all in competition to pass on their own characteristics to the next generation. This is how features of animals and plants that look as if they have been invented by an intelligent mind have come about.

Evolution is a mindless process. It has no consciousness or God behind it – or at least it doesn't *need* to have anything like this behind it. It is impersonal: like a machine that keeps working automatically. It is blind in the sense that it doesn't know where it is going and it doesn't think about the animals and plants that it produces. Nor does it care about them. When we see its products – plants and animals – it's difficult not to think of them as cleverly designed by someone. But that would be a mistake. Darwin's theory provides a much simpler and more elegant explanation. It also explains why there are so many types of life, with different species adapting to the parts of the environment they live in.

In 1858 Darwin still hadn't got round to publishing his findings. He was working on his book – he wanted to get it just right. Another naturalist, Alfred Russel Wallace (1823–1913), wrote to him sketching his own, very similar theory of evolution. This coincidence nudged Darwin into going public with his ideas, first with a presentation to the Linnean Society in London, and then the next year, 1859, with his book *On the Origin of Species*. After devoting a large part of his life to working out his theory, Darwin didn't want Wallace to get there before him. The book instantly made him famous.

Some people who read it were unconvinced. The captain of the *Beagle*, Robert FitzRoy, for example, a scientist himself and inventor of a system of weather forecasting, was a devout believer in the biblical story of Creation. He was dismayed that he had played a part in undermining religious belief, and wished he'd never taken Darwin on board his ship. Even today, there are creationists who believe that the story told in Genesis is true and a literal description of the origin of life. But among scientists there is overwhelming confidence that Darwin's theory explains the basic process of evolution. This is partly because since Darwin's time there has been a mass of new observations in support of the theory and of later versions of it. Genetics, for example, has given a detailed explanation of how inheritance works. We know about genes and chromosomes and about the chemical processes involved in passing on particular qualities. The fossil evidence today is also far more convincing than it was in Darwin's day. For all these reasons the theory of evolution by natural selection is much more than 'just a hypothesis': it is a hypothesis that has a very substantial weight of evidence in its support.

Darwinism may have more or less destroyed the traditional Design Argument and shaken many people's religious faith. But Darwin himself seems to have kept an open mind on the question of whether or not God exists. In a letter to a fellow scientist he declared that we aren't really up to coming to a conclusion on the issue: 'the whole subject is too profound for human intellect,' he explained: 'A dog might as well speculate on the mind of Newton.'

A thinker who was prepared to speculate about religious faith, and, unlike Darwin, made it central to his life's work, was Søren Kierkegaard.

CHAPTER 26

Life's Sacrifices
Søren Kierkegaard

Abraham has a message from God. It is a truly awful one: he must sacrifice his only son, Isaac. Abraham is in emotional torment. He loves his son, but he is also a devout man and knows he has to obey God. In this story from Genesis in the Old Testament, Abraham takes his son up to the top of a mountain, Mount Moriah, ties him to a stone altar and is about to kill him with a knife, as God has instructed. At the very last second, though, God sends an angel who stops the slaughter. Instead, Abraham sacrifices a ram that is caught in some bushes nearby. God rewards Abraham's loyalty by allowing his son to live.

This is a story with a message. The moral is usually thought to be, 'Have faith, do what God tells you to do and everything will turn out for the best.' The point is not to doubt God's word. But for the Danish philosopher Søren Kierkegaard (1813–55), it wasn't quite so simple. In his book *Fear and Trembling* (1842) he tried to imagine what must have gone through Abraham's mind, the questions, fears and anguish as he made the three-day journey from his home to the mountain where he believed he would have to kill Isaac.

Kierkegaard was quite odd and didn't fit in easily in Copenhagen where he lived. During the day this small thin man was often seen walking around the city deep in conversation with a companion and liked to think of himself as the Danish Socrates. He wrote in the evening – standing up in front of his desk surrounded by candles. One of his quirks was to show up at the interval of a play so that everyone thought he'd been out enjoying himself when he'd really not watched the play at all but had been busy at home writing for most of it. He worked very hard as a writer, but he had an agonizing choice to make in his personal life.

He had fallen in love with a young woman, Regine Olsen, and had asked her to marry him. She had agreed. But he worried that he was too gloomy and too religious to marry anyone. Perhaps he would live up to his family name 'Kierkegaard', which means 'graveyard' in Danish. He wrote to Regine telling her he couldn't marry her and returned his engagement ring. He felt terrible about his decision and spent many nights crying in bed after that. She, understandably, was devastated and begged him to come back. Kierkegaard refused. It is no coincidence that after that most of his writing was about choosing how to live and the difficulty of knowing that your decision is the right one.

Decision-making is built into the title of his most famous work: *Either/Or*. This book gives the reader a choice between *either* a life of pleasure and chasing after beauty *or* one based on conventional moral rules, a choice between the aesthetic and the ethical. But a theme he kept returning to throughout his writing was faith in God. The story of Abraham is at the heart of that. For Kierkegaard, it is not a simple decision to believe in God, but one that requires a kind of leap into the dark, a decision taken in faith that may even go against conventional ideas of what you should do.

If Abraham had gone ahead and killed his son he would have done something morally wrong. A father has a basic duty to look after his son, and certainly shouldn't tie him to an altar and cut his throat in a religious ritual. What God asked Abraham to do was to ignore morality and make a leap of faith. In the Bible Abraham is presented as admirable for ignoring this normal sense of right and wrong and being ready to sacrifice Isaac. But couldn't he have made a terrible mistake? What if the message wasn't really from God? Perhaps it was a hallucination; perhaps Abraham was insane and hearing voices. How could he know for sure? If he had known in advance that God wouldn't follow through on his command, it would have been easy for Abraham. But as he raised that knife ready to shed his son's blood, he really believed that he was going to kill him. That, as the Bible describes the scene, is the point. His faith is so impressive *because* he put his trust in God rather than in conventional ethical considerations. It wouldn't have been faith otherwise. Faith involves risk. But it is also irrational: not based on reason.

Kierkegaard believed that sometimes ordinary social duties, such as that a father should always protect his son, are not the highest values there can be. The duty to obey God trumps the duty to be a good father, and indeed any other duty. From a human perspective, Abraham might seem hard-hearted and immoral for even considering sacrificing his son. But it is as if God's command is an ace of trumps that wins the game, whatever it is that God commands. There is no higher card in the pack, and so human ethics are no longer relevant. Yet the person who abandons ethics in favour of faith makes an agonizing decision, risking everything, not knowing what benefit there could possibly be from doing so, or what will happen; not knowing for sure that the message is truly from God. Those who choose this path are totally alone.

Kierkegaard was a Christian, though he hated the Danish Church and couldn't accept the way complacent Christians around him behaved. For him, religion was a heart-wrenching option, not a cosy excuse for a song in church. In his opinion the Danish Church distorted Christianity and wasn't truly Christian. Not surprisingly, this didn't make him popular. Like Socrates, he ruffled the feathers of those around him who didn't like his criticisms and pointed remarks.

So far in this chapter I've written confidently about what Kierkegaard believed. But interpreting what he really meant in any of his books isn't easy. This was no accident. He is a writer who invites you to think for yourself. He rarely wrote under his own name, but instead used pseudonyms. For example, he wrote *Fear and Trembling* under the name Johannes de Silentio – John of Silence. This wasn't just a disguise to prevent people discovering that Kierkegaard had written the books – many people guessed who the author was straight away, which is probably what he wanted. The invented authors of his books are, rather, characters with their own way of looking at the world. This is one of Kierkegaard's techniques for getting you to understand the positions he is discussing and encouraging you to be engaged as you read. You see the world through that character's eyes and are left to make up your own mind about the value of their different approaches to life.

Reading Kierkegaard's writing is almost like reading a novel and he often uses fictional narrative to develop ideas.

In, *Either/Or* (1843), the imaginary editor of the book, Victor Eremita, describes finding a manuscript in a secret drawer in a second-hand desk. The manuscript is the main text of the book. It has supposedly been written by two different people – he describes them as A and B. The first is a pleasure-seeker whose life revolves around his avoidance of boredom by seeking new thrills. He tells the story of the seduction of a young woman in the form of a diary that reads like a short story and mirrors in some ways Kierkegaard's relationship with Regine. The pleasure-seeker, though, unlike Kierkegaard, is only interested in his own feelings. The second part of *Either/Or* is written as if by a judge who makes the case for a moral way of life. The style of the first part reflects A's interests: it consists of short pieces about art, opera and seduction. It's as if the author can't keep his mind on any one topic for long. The second half is written in a more sober and long-winded style that reflects the judge's outlook on life.

In case you are feeling sorry for poor jilted Regine Olsen, by the way, after her difficult on–off relationship with Kierkegaard she married a civil servant and seems to have been happy enough for the rest of her life. Kierkegaard, however, never married, never even had a girlfriend after their break-up. She really was his true love and their failed relationship was the source of almost everything that he wrote in his short and tormented life.

Like many philosophers, Kierkegaard wasn't fully appreciated during his brief lifetime – he died aged only 42. In the twentieth century, however, his books became popular with existentialists such as Jean-Paul Sartre (see Chapter 33) who were particularly taken with his ideas about the anguish of choosing what to do in the absence of pre-existing guidelines.

For Kierkegaard, the subjective point of view, the experience of the individual making choices, was all-important. Karl Marx took a broader view. Like Hegel, he had a grand vision of how history was unfolding and of the forces driving it. Unlike Kierkegaard, he saw no hope whatsoever of salvation through religion.

CHAPTER 27

Workers of the World Unite
KARL MARX

In the nineteenth century there were thousands of cotton mills in the north of England. Dark smoke poured from their tall chimneys, polluting the streets and covering everything in soot. Inside men, women and children worked very long hours – often 14-hour days – to keep the spinning machines going. They weren't quite slaves, but their wages were very low, and the conditions were tough and often dangerous. If they lost concentration they could get caught up in the machinery and lose limbs or even be killed. Medical treatment in these circumstances was basic. They had little choice, though: if they didn't work they would starve. If they walked away, they might not find another job. People who worked in these conditions didn't live long, and there were very few moments in their lives they could call their own.

Meanwhile the owners of the mills grew rich. Their main concern was making a profit. They owned capital (money they could put to use to make more money); they owned the buildings and the machinery; and they more or less owned the workers. The workers had next to nothing. All they could do was sell their ability to work and help the mill owners grow rich. By their labour they added value to the raw materials that the mill owners bought. When the cotton came into the factory it was worth much less than it was when it left. But that added value mostly went to the owners when they sold the product. As for the workers, the factory owners paid them as little as possible – often just what would keep them alive. The workers had no job security. If demand for whatever they were making declined, they were sacked and left to die if they couldn't find more work. When the German philosopher Karl Marx (1818–83) began writing in the 1830s these were the grim conditions that the Industrial Revolution had produced not just in England, but all over Europe. It made him angry.

Marx was an egalitarian: he thought human beings should be treated equally. But in the capitalist system those who had money – often from inherited wealth – got richer and richer. Meanwhile those who had nothing but their labour to sell lived wretched lives and were exploited. For Marx, the whole of human history could be explained as a class struggle: the struggle between the rich capitalist class (the bourgeoisie) and the working class or proletariat. This relationship stopped human beings achieving their potential and turned work into something painful rather than a fulfilling kind of activity.

Marx, a man of immense energy and with a reputation for causing trouble, spent most of his life in poverty, moving from Germany to Paris, then Brussels to avoid persecution. Eventually he made his home in London. There he lived with his seven children, his wife Jenny, and a housekeeper Helene Demuth with whom he had an illegitimate child. His friend Friedrich

Engels helped him find work writing for newspapers and even adopted Marx's illegitimate son to help him save face. But the Marx family rarely had enough money. They were often sick, hungry and cold. Tragically, three of his children died before reaching adulthood.

In later life, most days Marx would walk to the Reading Room at the British Museum in London and study and write, or else stay at home in his crowded Soho flat and dictate to his wife because his own handwriting was so bad that sometimes even he couldn't read it. In these difficult conditions he produced a huge number of books and articles – they fill more than fifty thick volumes. His ideas have changed the lives of millions of people, some for the better, and many, undoubtedly, for the worse. At the time, though, he must have seemed an eccentric figure, perhaps a little crazy. Few people could have foreseen how influential he would be.

Marx identified with the workers. The whole structure of society ground them down. They couldn't live fully as human beings. Factory owners very soon realized that they could make more goods if they broke the production process down into small tasks. Each worker could then specialize in a particular job on the production line. But this made the workers' lives even more tedious as they were forced to perform boring, repetitive actions over and over again. They didn't see the whole process of production and they barely earned enough to feed themselves. Instead of being creative, they were worn down and turned into cogs in a huge piece of machinery that was there just to make the factory owners richer. It was as if they weren't really human beings at all – just stomachs that needed to be fed to keep the production line going and the capitalists extracting more profit: what Marx called the surplus value created by the workers' labour.

The effect on the workers of all this was what Marx labelled *alienation.* He meant several things by this word. The workers were alienated or distanced from what they truly were as human beings. The things they made alienated them too. The harder the workers worked and the more they produced, the more profit they made for the capitalists. The objects themselves seemed to take revenge on the workers.

But there was some hope for these people even though their lives were miserable and completely mapped out by economic circumstances. Marx believed that capitalism would in the end destroy itself. The proletariat was destined to take over in a violent revolution. Eventually from all this bloodshed a better world would emerge, one in which people were no longer exploited, but could be creative and co-operate with each other. Each person would contribute whatever they could to society, and society in turn would provide for them: 'from each according to his ability, to each according to his need' was Marx's vision. By taking control of factories, the workers would make sure that there was enough for everyone to have what they needed. No one need go hungry or without suitable clothing or shelter. This future was communism, a world based on sharing the benefits of co-operation.

Marx believed that his study of the way society develops revealed that this future was inevitable. It was built into the structure of history. But it could be helped along a bit, and in the *Communist Manifesto* of 1848, which he wrote with Engels, he called upon workers of the world to unite and overthrow capitalism. Echoing the opening lines of Jean-Jacques Rousseau's *Social Contract* (see Chapter 18), they declared that the workers had nothing to lose but their chains.

Marx's ideas about history were influenced by Hegel (the subject of Chapter 22). Hegel, as we have seen, declared that there is an underlying structure to everything, and that we are gradually progressing to a world that will somehow be conscious of itself. Marx took from Hegel the sense that progress is inevitable, and that history has a pattern and is not just one thing after another. But in Marx's version, progress occurs because of the underlying economic forces.

In place of the class struggle Marx and Engels promised a world in which no one would own land, where there was no inheritance, where education was free, and where public factories provided for everyone. There would be no need for religion or morality either. Religion, he famously declared, was 'the opium of the people': it was like a drug keeping them in a sleepy state so they didn't realize their true oppressed condition. In the new world after the revolution human beings would achieve their humanity. Their work would be meaningful and they would co-operate in ways that benefited everyone. Revolution was the way to achieve all this – and this meant violence, since the rich were unlikely to give up their wealth without a struggle.

Marx felt that philosophers of the past had only described the world, whereas he wanted to change it. This was a little unfair to earlier philosophers, many of whom had brought about moral and political reform. But his ideas had more effect than most. They were contagious, inspiring real revolutions in Russia in 1917 and elsewhere. Unfortunately the Soviet Union – the huge state that emerged, embracing Russia and some of its neighbours – together with most other communist states created in the twentieth century on Marxist lines, proved oppressive, inefficient and corrupt. Organizing the processes of production on a national scale was far harder than might be imagined. Marxists claim that this doesn't damage Marxist ideas themselves – some still believe that Marx was basically right about society, it's just that those who ran the communist states didn't run them on truly communist lines. Others point out that human nature makes us more competitive and greedy for ourselves than he allowed: there is no possibility in their view of human beings co-operating fully in a communist state – we're just not like that.

When he died of tuberculosis in 1883, few people could have foreseen Marx's impact on later history. It looked as if his ideas would be buried with him in London's Highgate Cemetery. Engels' declaration at the graveside that 'His name will endure through the ages, and so also will his work!' seemed like wishful thinking.

Marx's main interest was in economic relationships since in his view they shape everything that we are and can become. William James, a pragmatist philosopher, meant something quite different when he wrote about the 'cash value' of an idea – for him, that was simply what action the idea led to, what difference it made in the world.

So What?

C.S. Peirce and William James

A squirrel is clinging tightly to the trunk of a large tree. On the other side of the tree, close up against the trunk is a hunter. Every time the hunter moves to his left, the squirrel moves quickly to its left too, scurrying further round the trunk, hanging on with its claws. The hunter keeps trying to find the squirrel, but it manages to keep just out of his sight. This goes on for hours, and the hunter never gets a glimpse of the squirrel. Would it be true to say that the hunter is *circling* the squirrel? Think about it. Does the hunter actually *circle* his prey?

It's possible that your answer will be 'Why do you want to know?' The American philosopher and psychologist William James (1842–1910) came across a group of friends arguing about this same example. He would have had some sympathy with your response. His friends couldn't agree on the answer but were discussing the question as if there were an absolute truth to the matter that they could uncover. Some said yes, the hunter *was* circling the squirrel; others said no, he certainly wasn't. They thought James might be able to help them answer the question one way or the other. His response was based on his *pragmatist* philosophy.

This is what he said. If you mean by circling that the man is first north, then east, then south, then west of the squirrel, which is one meaning of 'circling', then the answer is that it is true that the hunter circles the squirrel. He does go round the squirrel in this sense. But if you mean that the hunter is first of all in front of the squirrel, then to the squirrel's right, then behind the squirrel and then to its left, another meaning of 'circling', then the answer is no. Because the squirrel's belly is always facing the hunter, the hunter doesn't go round the squirrel in that sense. They are always face to face with each other with the tree in between them as they dance round out of each other's sight.

The point of this example is to show that pragmatism is concerned with practical consequences – the 'cash value' of thought. If nothing hangs on the answer, it doesn't really matter what you decide. It all depends why you want to know and what difference it will actually make. Here, there is no truth beyond particular human concerns with the question, and the precise ways we use the verb 'to circle' in different contexts. If there is no practical difference, then there is no truth of the matter. It's not that truth is somehow 'out there' waiting for us to find it. Truth for James was simply what works, what has a beneficial impact on our lives.

Pragmatism is a philosophical approach that became popular in the United States in the late nineteenth century. It started with the American philosopher and scientist C.S. Peirce (pronounced 'purse'), who wanted to make philosophy more scientific than it had been. Peirce (1839–1914) believed that for a statement to be true there had to be some possible experiment or observation to support it. If you say 'Glass is brittle' what this means is that if you hit it with a hammer it will break into tiny fragments. That's what makes the statement 'Glass is brittle' true. There isn't some invisible property of 'brittleness' the glass has apart from this fact about what happens if you hit it. 'Glass is brittle' is a true statement because of these practical consequences. 'Glass is transparent' is true because you can see through glass, not because of some mysterious property in the glass. Peirce hated abstract theories that didn't make any difference in practice. He thought they were nonsense. Truth for him is what we would end up with if we could run all the experiments and investigations we would ideally like to. This is very close to A.J. Ayer's logical positivism which is the subject of Chapter 32.

Peirce's work was not widely read. But William James' was. He was an excellent writer – as good as or better than his famous brother, the novelist and short story writer Henry James. William had spent many hours discussing pragmatism with Peirce when they had both been lecturers at Harvard University. James developed his own version of it that he popularized in essays and lectures. For him, pragmatism boils down to this: truth is what works. He was, though, a bit vague about what 'what works' meant. Although he was an early psychologist, he wasn't interested just in science, but also in questions about right and wrong, and religion too. In fact his most controversial writing was about religion.

James' approach is very different from the traditional view of truth. On that view truth means correspondence to the facts. What makes a sentence true on the correspondence theory of truth is that it accurately describes how the world is. 'The cat is on the mat' is true when the cat is actually sitting on the mat, and false when it isn't; when, for example, it is out in the garden looking for mice. According to James' pragmatic theory of truth, what makes the sentence 'The cat is on the mat' true is that believing it produces useful practical results for us. It works for us. So, for example, believing 'the cat is on the mat' gives the result that we know not to play with our pet hamster on that mat until the cat has gone somewhere else.

Now, when using an example like 'The cat is on the mat', the results of this pragmatic theory of truth don't seem particularly disconcerting or important. But try it with the sentence 'God exists.' What would you expect James to say about that?

Is it true that God exists? What do you think? The main answers are 'Yes, it's true that God exists', 'No it's not true that God exists', and 'I don't know.' Presumably you gave one of those answers if you bothered to answer my question before reading this. These positions have names: theism, atheism and agnosticism. Those who say 'Yes, it's true that God exists' usually mean that there is a Supreme Being somewhere and that the statement 'God exists' would be true even if there were no human beings alive and even if no human beings had ever existed. 'God exists' and 'God doesn't exist' are statements that are either true or false. But it's not what we think about them that makes them true or false. They are true or false whatever we think about them. We just hope we get it right when we think about them.

James gave a rather different analysis of 'God exists.' He thought that the statement was true. What made it true was that it was in his opinion a useful belief to have. In coming to that conclusion he focused on the benefits of believing that God exists. This was an important issue for him and he wrote a book, *The Varieties of Religious Experience* (1902), which examined a wide range of effects that religious belief can have. For James, to say that 'God exists' is a true statement is simply to say that it is somehow good for the believer to believe it. This is quite a surprising position to take. It's a bit like Pascal's argument that we looked at in Chapter 12: that agnostics stood to benefit from believing that God existed. Pascal, though, believed that 'God exists' was made true by the real existence of God, not by human beings feeling better when they believe in God, or becoming better people because they have this belief. His Wager was just a way of getting agnostics to believe what he thought was true. For James, it is the supposed fact that belief in God 'works satisfactorily' that makes 'God exists' true.

To get clear about this, take the sentence 'Santa Claus exists.' Is that true? Does a large, jolly red-faced man come down your chimney every Christmas Eve with a sack of presents? Don't read the rest of this paragraph if you believe that this does actually happen. I'm guessing, though, that you *don't* think Santa Claus exists even if you think that it would be nice if he did. The British philosopher Bertrand Russell (see Chapter 31) made fun of William James' pragmatic theory of truth by saying it meant that James had to believe 'Santa Claus exists' is true. His reason for saying this was that James thinks that all that makes a sentence true is the effect on the believer of believing it. And for most children, at least, believing in Santa Claus is great. It makes Christmas a very special day for them; it makes them behave well; it gives them a focus in the days coming up to Christmas. It works for them. So because believing it works in some sense, that seems to make it true according to James' theory. The trouble is there is a difference between what would be nice if it were true and what is actually true. James could have pointed out that while believing in Santa Claus works for young children, it doesn't work for everyone. If parents believed that Santa was going to deliver presents on Christmas Eve then they wouldn't go out and buy presents for their children. It would only take until Christmas morning to realize that something wasn't working with the belief 'Santa Claus exists'. But does that mean it's true for small children that Santa Claus exists, but false for most adults? And doesn't that make truth subjective, a matter of how we feel about things rather than the way the world is?

Take another example. How do I know that other people have minds at all? I know from my own experience that I'm not just some kind of a zombie with no internal life. I have my own thoughts, intentions and so forth. But how can I tell whether people around me have thoughts at all? Perhaps they aren't conscious. Couldn't they just be zombies acting automatically with no minds of their own? This is the Problem of Other Minds that philosophers have worried about for a long time. It is a difficult puzzle to solve. James' answer was that it must be true that other people have minds, otherwise we wouldn't be able to satisfy our desire to be recognized and admired by other people. This is an odd sort of argument. It makes his pragmatism sound very much like wishful thinking – believing what you'd like to be true whether or not it is actually true. But just because it feels good to believe that when someone praises you they are a conscious being and not a robot doesn't make them a conscious being. They could still lack any internal life.

In the twentieth century the American philosopher Richard Rorty (1931–2007) carried on this style of pragmatic thinking. Like James, he thought of words as tools that we do things with, rather than symbols that somehow mirror the way the world is. Words allow us to cope with the world, not copy it. He declared that 'truth is what your contemporaries let you get away with' and that no period of history gets reality more nearly right than any other. When people describe the world, Rorty believed, they are like literary critics giving an interpretation of a Shakespeare play: there's no single 'correct' way of reading it that we should all agree on. Different people at different times interpret the text differently. Rorty simply rejected the idea that any one view is correct for all time. Or at least that's my interpretation of his work. Rorty presumably believed that there was no correct interpretation of it in the same way that there's no 'right' answer about whether the hunter was circling the squirrel as it scrambled round the tree.

Whether or not there is a correct interpretation of the writings of Friedrich Nietzsche is also an interesting question.

CHAPTER 29

The Death of God
FRIEDRICH NIETZSCHE

'God is dead'. These are the most famous words that the German philosopher Friedrich Nietzsche (1844–1900) wrote. But how could God die? God is supposed to be immortal. Immortal beings don't die. They live for ever. In a way, though, that's the point. That's why God's death sounds so odd: it's meant to. Nietzsche was deliberately playing on the idea that God couldn't die. He wasn't literally saying that God had been alive at one time and now wasn't; rather that belief in God had stopped being reasonable. In his book *Joyful Wisdom* (1882) Nietzsche put the line 'God is dead' in the mouth of a character who holds a lantern and looks everywhere for God, but can't find him. The villagers think he is crazy.

Nietzsche was a remarkable man. Appointed as a professor at the University of Basel at the very young age of 24, he looked set for a distinguished academic career. But this eccentric and original thinker didn't fit in or conform, and seemed to enjoy making life hard for himself. He eventually left the university in 1879, partly because of ill health, and travelled in Italy, France and Switzerland, writing books that hardly anyone read at the time, but which are now famous as works of both philosophy and literature. His psychological health declined and he spent much of his later life in an asylum.

In complete contrast to Immanuel Kant's orderly presentation of ideas, Nietzsche's come at you from all angles. Much of the writing is in the form of short, fragmentary paragraphs and pithy one-sentence comments, some of them ironic, some sincere, many of them arrogant and provocative. Sometimes it feels as if Nietzsche is shouting at you, sometimes that he is whispering something profound in your ear. Often he wants the reader to collude with him, as if he is saying that you and I know how things are, but those foolish people over there are all suffering from delusions. One theme he keeps returning to is the future of morality.

If God is dead, what comes next? That's the question Nietzsche asked himself. His answer was that it left us without a basis for morality. Our ideas of right and wrong and good and evil make sense in a world where there is a God. They don't in a godless one. Take away God and you take away the possibility of clear guidelines about how we should live, which things to value. That's a tough message, and not one most of his contemporaries wanted to hear. He described himself as an 'immoralist', not someone who deliberately does evil, but someone who believes that we need to get beyond all morality: in the words of the title of one of his books, 'beyond good and evil'.

For Nietzsche, the death of God opened up new possibilities for humanity. These were both terrifying and exhilarating. The downside was that there was no safety net, no rules about how people had to live or be. Where once religion had provided meaning and a limit on moral action, the absence of God made everything possible and removed all limits. The upside, at least from Nietzsche's perspective, was that individuals could now create their own values for themselves. They could turn their lives into the equivalent of works of art by developing their own style of living.

Nietzsche saw that once you accept there is no God, you can't just cling to a Christian view of right and wrong. That would be self-deception. The values that his culture had inherited, values such as compassion, kindness, and consideration of other people's interests, could all be challenged. His way of doing this was to speculate about where these values originally came from.

According to Nietzsche, the Christian virtues of looking after the weak and helpless had surprising origins. You might think that compassion and kindness are obviously good. You've probably been brought up to praise kindness and despise selfishness. What Nietzsche claimed is that the patterns of thought and feeling that we happen to possess have a history. Once you know the history or 'genealogy' of how we come to have the concepts that we do, it is hard to think of them as fixed for all time and as somehow objective facts about how we ought to behave.

In his book *The Genealogy of Morality* he described the situation in Ancient Greece when powerful aristocratic heroes built their lives around ideas of honour, shame and heroism in battle rather than kindness, generosity and guilt at wrongdoing. This is the world described by the Greek poet Homer in the *Odyssey* and the *Iliad*. In this world of heroes, those who were powerless, the slaves and the weak, were envious of the powerful. The slaves channelled their envy and resentment towards the powerful. Out of these negative feelings they created a new set of values. They turned the heroic values of the aristocrats on their head. Instead of celebrating strength and power like the aristocrats, the slaves made generosity and care for the weak into virtues. This slave morality, as Nietzsche calls it, treated the acts of the powerful as evil and their own fellow feelings as good.

The idea that a morality of kindness had its beginnings in feelings of envy was a challenging one. Nietzsche showed a strong preference for the values of the aristocrats, the celebration of strong warlike heroes, over the Christian morality of compassion for the weak. Christianity and the morality derived from it treats every individual as having the same worth; Nietzsche thought that was a serious mistake. His artistic heroes like Beethoven and Shakespeare were far superior to the herd. The message seems to be that Christian values, which emerged from envy in the first place, were holding humanity back. The cost might be that the weak get trampled on, but that was a price worth paying for the glory and achievement that this opened up for the powerful.

In *Thus Spake Zaruthustra* (1883–92) he wrote about the *Übermensch* or 'Super-Man'. This describes an imagined person of the future who is not held back by conventional moral codes, but goes beyond them, creating new values. Perhaps influenced by his understanding of Charles Darwin's theory of evolution, he saw the *Übermensch* as the next step in humanity's development. This is a bit worrying, partly because it seems to support those who see themselves as heroic and want to have their way without consideration of other people's interests. Worse still, it was an idea that the Nazis took from Nietzsche's work and used to support their warped views about a master race, though most scholars argue that they distorted what Nietzsche actually wrote.

Nietzsche was unfortunate in that his sister Elisabeth controlled what happened to his work after he lost his sanity and for thirty-five years after his death. She was a German nationalist of the very worst kind and an anti-Semite. She went through her brother's notebooks, picking out the lines she agreed with and leaving out anything that criticized Germany or didn't support her racist viewpoint. Her cut-and-paste version of Nietzsche's ideas, published as *The Will to Power*, turned his writing into propaganda for Nazism, and Nietzsche became an approved author in the Third Reich. It is highly unlikely that, had he lived longer, he would have had anything to do with it. Yet it is undeniable that there are plenty of lines in his work that defend the right of the strong to destroy the weak. It is no surprise, he tells us, that lambs hate birds of prey. But that doesn't mean we should despise the birds of prey for carrying off and devouring the lambs.

Unlike Immanuel Kant, who celebrated reason, Nietzsche always emphasized how emotions and irrational forces play their part in shaping human values. His views almost certainly influenced Sigmund Freud, whose work explored the nature and power of unconscious desires.

CHAPTER 30

Thoughts in Disguise
SIGMUND FREUD

Can you really know yourself? The Ancient philosophers believed that you could. But what if they were wrong? What if there are parts of your mind that you can never reach directly, like rooms that are permanently locked so that you can never enter them?

Appearances can be deceptive. When you watch the sun in the early morning it seems to come up from beyond the horizon. During the day it moves across the sky and then finally sets. It is tempting to think that it travels around the earth. For many centuries people were convinced it did. But it doesn't. In the sixteenth century the astronomer Nicolaus Copernicus realized this, though other astronomers had their suspicions before that. The Copernican revolution, the idea that our planet was not at the heart of the solar system, came as a shock.

The mid-nineteenth century brought another surprise, as we have seen (Chapter 25). Until then it had seemed likely that human beings were completely different from animals and had been designed by God. But Charles Darwin's theory of evolution by natural selection showed that human beings share common ancestors with apes and that there was no need to suppose that God had designed us. An impersonal process was responsible. Darwin's theory explained how we had descended from ape-like creatures and how close we were to them. The effects of the Darwinian revolution are still being felt.

According to Sigmund Freud (1856–1939), the third great revolution in human thought was brought about by his own discovery: the unconscious. He realized that much of what we do is driven by wishes that are hidden from us. We can't get at them directly. But that doesn't stop them affecting what we do. There are things that we want to do that we don't realize we want to do. These unconscious desires have a deep influence on all our lives and on the way we organize society. They are the source of the best and worst aspects of human civilization. Freud was responsible for this discovery, though a similar idea can be found in some of Friedrich Nietzsche's writing.

Freud, a psychiatrist who had begun his career as a neurologist, lived in Vienna when Austria was still part of the Austro-Hungarian Empire. The son of a middle-class Jewish father, he was typical of many well-educated and established young men in this cosmopolitan city at the end of the nineteenth century. His work with several young patients, however, drew his attention increasingly to the parts of the psyche that he believed were governing their behaviour, creating their problems through mechanisms of which they were unaware. He was fascinated by hysteria and other types of neurosis. These hysterical patients, who were mostly women, often walked in their sleep, hallucinated, and even developed paralysis. Yet it wasn't known what was causing all this. Doctors couldn't find a physical cause for these symptoms. Through careful attention to the patients' descriptions of their problems and knowledge of their personal histories, Freud came up with the idea that the real source of these people's problems was some kind of disturbing memory or desire. This memory or desire was unconscious and they had no idea that they had it.

Freud would get his patients to lie on a couch and talk about whatever came into their head, and often this made them feel much better as it let their ideas escape. This 'free association', allowing the ideas to flow, produced surprising results, making what was previously unconscious conscious. He also asked patients to recount their dreams. Somehow this 'talking cure' unlocked their troublesome thoughts and removed some of the symptoms. It was as if the act of talking released pressure caused by the ideas they did not want to confront. This was the birth of psychoanalysis.

But it isn't just neurotic and hysterical patients who have unconscious wishes and memories. According to Freud, we all do. That is how life in society is possible. We hide from ourselves what we really feel and want to do. Some of these thoughts are violent and many are sexual. They are too dangerous to let out. The mind *represses* them, keeps them down in the unconscious. Many are formed when we are small children. Very early events in a child's life can re-emerge in adulthood. For example, Freud believed that men all have an unconscious wish to kill their father and have sex with their mother. This is the famous Oedipus complex, named after Oedipus who in Greek mythology fulfilled the prophecy that he would murder his father and marry his mother (without being aware in either case that he was doing so). For some people, this early awkward desire completely shapes their life without them even realizing it. Something in the mind stops these darker thoughts getting through in a recognizable form. But whatever it is in us that stops this, and other unconscious desires, from becoming conscious isn't completely successful. The thoughts still manage to escape, but in disguise. They emerge in dreams, for example.

For Freud, dreams were 'the royal road to the unconscious', one of the best ways of finding out about hidden thoughts. The things we see and experience in dreams aren't what they seem. There is the surface content, what appears to be going on. But the *latent* content is the real meaning of the dream. That is what the psychoanalyst tries to understand. The things we encounter in dreams are symbols. They stand for the wishes that lurk in our unconscious minds. So, for example, a dream that involves a snake or an umbrella or a sword is usually a disguised sexual dream. The snake, umbrella and sword are classic 'Freudian symbols' – they stand for a penis. Similarly in a dream the image of a purse or a cave represents a vagina. If you find this idea shocking and absurd, Freud would probably tell you that that is because your mind is protecting you from recognizing such sexual thoughts within yourself.

Another way in which we get glimpses of unconscious wishes is in slips of the tongue, so-called Freudian slips, where we accidentally reveal wishes that we don't realize we have. Many television newsreaders have stumbled over a name or phrase, accidentally speaking an obscenity. A Freudian would say this happens too often for it simply to be a matter of chance.

Not all unconscious wishes are sexual or violent. Some reveal a fundamental conflict. On a conscious level we may want one thing that on an unconscious level we do not want. Imagine you have an important examination that you have to pass in order to go to university. Consciously you do everything in your power to prepare for it. You go through the relevant past examination papers, prepare the answers to the questions in outline form and make sure you set your alarm clock early to get to the examination room on time. Everything seems to be going well. You wake up on time, eat breakfast, catch the bus, and realize you will arrive with time to spare. At this point you doze off contentedly on the bus. But when you awake you find, to your horror, that you have misread the number on the bus and are now in completely the wrong part of town with no chance of getting to the right part in time to sit the examination. Your fear of the consequences of passing the examination seem to have overruled your conscious efforts. At a deep level you didn't want to succeed. It would be too frightening to admit this to yourself, but your unconscious revealed it to you.

Freud applied his theory not just to individuals acting neurotically, but also to common cultural beliefs. In particular he gave a psychoanalytic account of why people are so drawn to religion. You might believe in God. Perhaps you feel God's presence in your life. But Freud had an explanation for where your belief in God comes from. You might think you believe in God because God exists, but Freud thought that you believe in God because you still feel the need for protection that you felt as a very small child. In Freud's view whole civilizations have been based on this illusion – the illusion that there is a strong father-figure out there somewhere who will meet your unmet needs for protection. This is wishful thinking – believing that such a God really exists because you have a great desire in your heart that he should. It all stems from the unconscious desire to be protected and cared for that arises in early childhood. The idea of God is comforting for adults who still have these feelings left over from childhood, even though they don't usually realize where the feelings came from and actively repress the idea that their religion comes entirely from a deeply felt and unmet psychological need rather than from the existence of God.

From a philosophical point of view, Freud's work brought into question many assumptions that thinkers such as René Descartes had made about the mind. Descartes believed that the mind was transparent to itself. He believed that if you have a thought you must be able to be aware of that thought. After Freud the possibility of unconscious mental activity had to be acknowledged.

But the basis of Freud's ideas aren't accepted by all philosophers, though many accept that he was right about the possibility of unconscious thought. Some have claimed that Freud's theories are unscientific. Most famously, Karl Popper (whose ideas are more fully discussed in Chapter 36) described many of the ideas of psychoanalysis as 'unfalsifiable'. This wasn't a compliment, but a criticism. For Popper, the essence of scientific research was that it could be tested; that is, there could be some possible observation that would show that it was false. In Popper's example, the actions of a man who pushed a child into a river, and a man who dived in to save a drowning child were, like all human behaviour, equally open to Freudian explanation. Whether someone tried to drown or save a child, Freud's theory could explain it. He would probably say that the first man was repressing some aspect of his Oedipal conflict, and that led to his violent behaviour, whereas the second man had 'sublimated' his unconscious desires, that is, managed to steer them into socially useful actions. If every possible observation is taken as further evidence that the theory is true, whatever that observation is, and no imaginable evidence could show that it was false, Popper believed, the theory couldn't be scientific at all. Freud, on the other hand, might have argued that Popper had some kind of repressed desire that made him so aggressive towards psychoanalysis.

Bertrand Russell, a very different style of thinker from Freud, shared his distaste for religion, believing that it was a major source of human unhappiness.

CHAPTER 31

Is the Present King of France Bald?
BERTRAND RUSSELL

Bertrand Russell's main interests as a teenager were sex, religion and mathematics – all at a theoretical level. In his very long life (he died in 1970, aged 97) he ended up being controversial about the first, attacking the second, and making important contributions to the third.

Russell's views on sex got him into trouble. In 1929 he published *Marriage and Morals*. In that book he questioned Christian views about the importance of being faithful to your partner. He didn't think you had to be. This raised a few eyebrows at the time. Not that that bothered Russell much. He'd already spent six months in Brixton prison for speaking out against the First World War in 1916. In later life he helped found the Campaign for Nuclear Disarmament (CND), which is an international movement opposed to all weapons of mass destruction. This sprightly old man would be at the front of public rallies in the 1960s, still as opposed to war as he had been as a young man some fifty years earlier. As he put it, 'Either man will abolish war, or war will abolish man.' So far neither outcome has been realized.

On religion he was just as outspoken and just as provocative. For Russell there was no chance of God stepping in to save humanity: our only chance lay in using our powers of reason. People were drawn to religion, he believed, because they were afraid of dying. Religion comforted them. It was very reassuring to believe that a God exists who will punish evil people, even if they get away with murder and worse on earth. But it wasn't true. God doesn't exist. And religion nearly always produced more misery than happiness. He did allow that Buddhism might be different from most other religions, but Christianity, Islam, Judaism and Hinduism all had a lot to answer for. These religions throughout their histories had been the cause of war, individual suffering and hatred. Millions had died as a result of them.

It should be clear from all this that, despite being a pacifist, Russell was prepared to stand up and fight (at least with ideas) for what he believed to be right and just. Even as a pacifist he still thought that in rare cases, such as the Second World War, fighting might be the best option available.

By birth he was an English aristocrat. He came from a very distinguished family: his official title was the 3rd Earl Russell. You could probably tell that he was an aristocrat just by looking at him. He had a distinguished haughty sort of look, an impish grin and twinkly eyes. His voice gave him away as a member of the upper classes. On recordings he sounds like something from another century – which he was: he was born in 1872, so was truly a Victorian. His grand-father on his father's side, Lord John Russell, had been Prime Minister.

Bertrand's non-religious 'godfather' was the philosopher John Stuart Mill (the subject of Chapter 24). Sadly, he never got to know him as Mill died when Russell was still a toddler. But he was still a huge influence on Russell's development. Reading Mill's *Autobiography* (1873) was what led Russell to reject God. He had previously believed the First Cause Argument. This is the argument, used by Thomas Aquinas amongst others, that everything must have a cause; and the cause of everything, the very first cause in the chain of cause and effect, must be God. But Mill asked the question 'What caused God?' and Russell saw the logical problem for the First Cause Argument. If there is one thing that doesn't have a cause then it can't be true that 'Everything has a cause'. It made more sense to Russell to think that even God had a cause rather than believe that something could just exist without being caused by anything else.

Like Mill, Russell had an unusual and not particularly happy childhood. Both his parents died when he was very young, and his grandmother, who looked after him, was strict and a bit distant. Taught at home by private tutors, he threw himself into his studies and became a brilliant mathematician, going on to lecture at Cambridge University. But what really fascinated him was what made mathematics true. Why is $2 + 2 = 4$ true? We know it is true. But why is it true? This led him quite quickly to philosophy.

As a philosopher, his real love was logic: a subject on the border between philosophy and mathematics. Logicians study the structure of reasoning, usually using symbols to express their ideas. He became fascinated by the branch of mathematics and logic called set theory. Set theory seemed to promise a way of explaining the structure of all our reasoning, but Russell came up with a big problem for that idea: it led to contradiction.

The way he showed this was in a famous paradox that was named after him.

Here's an example of Russell's Paradox. Imagine a village in which there is a barber whose job it is to shave all (and only) the people who don't shave themselves. If I lived there, I'd probably shave myself – I don't think I'd be organized enough to get to the barber every day and I can shave myself perfectly well. And it would probably work out too expensive for me. But if I decided I didn't want to, then the barber would be the one to shave me. But where does that leave the barber? He's allowed to shave only people who don't shave themselves. By this rule, he can't ever shave *himself* because he can only shave people who don't shave themselves. This is going to get difficult for him. Usually if someone can't shave himself in this village it is the barber who does it for him. But the rule won't allow the barber to do that, because that would turn him into someone who shaved himself – but the barber only shaves the ones who don't shave themselves.

This is a situation that seems to lead to a direct contradiction – saying something is both true and false. That's what a paradox is. It's very puzzling. What Russell discovered was that when a set refers to itself this sort of paradox emerges. Take another famous example of the same sort of thing: 'This sentence is false.' This is a paradox too. If the words 'This sentence is false' mean what they seem to mean (and are true) then the sentence is false – which then means that what it states is true! This seems to suggest that the sentence is both true and false. But a sentence can't be true and false at the same time. That's a basic part of logic. So there's the paradox.

These are interesting puzzles in themselves. There's no easy solution to them, and that seems strange. But they were far more important than that for Russell. What they did was reveal that some of the basic assumptions that logicians all over the world had been making about set theory were wrong. They needed to begin again.

Another of Russell's main interests was how what we say relates to the world. If he could work out what made a statement true or false it would be a significant contribution to human knowledge, he felt. Again, he was interested in the very abstract questions that lie behind all our thinking. Much of his work was devoted to explaining the logical structure underlying the statements we make. He felt that our language was far less precise than logic. Ordinary language needed to be analysed – taken apart – to bring out its underlying logical shape. He was convinced that the key to making advances in all areas of philosophy was this sort of logical analysis of language, which involved translating it into more precise terms.

For example, take the sentence, 'The golden mountain does not exist.' Everyone is likely to agree that this sentence is true. That's because there is no mountain made of gold anywhere in the world. The sentence seems to be saying something about a thing that does not exist. The phrase 'the golden mountain' seems to refer to something real, but we know it doesn't. This is a puzzle for logicians. How can we talk meaningfully about non-existent things? Why isn't the sentence completely meaningless? One answer, given by the Austrian logician Alexius Meinong, was that everything that we can think about and talk about meaningfully *does* exist. On his view, the golden mountain must exist, but in a special way he labelled 'subsistence'. He also thought unicorns and the number 27 'subsist' in this way.

Meinong's way of thinking about logic didn't seem right to Russell. It does seem very strange. It meant that the world was full of things that exist in one sense but not in another. Russell devised a simpler way of explaining how what we say relates to what exists. This is known as his Theory of Descriptions. Take the rather odd sentence (one of Russell's favourites) 'The present king of France is bald.' Even in the early twentieth century when Russell was writing there was no king of France. France got rid of all her kings and queens during the French Revolution. So how could he make sense of that sentence? Russell's answer was that, like most sentences in ordinary language, it wasn't quite what it seemed.

Here's the problem. If we want to say that the sentence 'The present king of France is bald' is false, this seems to be committing us to saying that there is a present king of France who isn't bald. But that surely isn't what we mean at all. We don't believe there is a present king of France. Russell's analysis was this. A statement like 'The present king of France is bald' is actually a kind of hidden description. When we speak about 'the present king of France' the underlying logical shape of our idea is this:

(a) There exists something that is the present king of France.
(b) There is only one thing that is the present king of France.
(c) Anything that is the present king of France is bald.

This complicated way of spelling things out allowed Russell to show that 'The present king of France is bald' can make some sense even though there is no present king of France. It makes sense, but is false. Unlike Meinong, he didn't need to imagine that the present king of France had to exist somehow (or subsist) in order to speak and think about him. For Russell the sentence 'The present king of France is bald' is false because the present king of France doesn't exist. The sentence suggests that he does; so the sentence is false rather than true. The sentence 'The present king of France is *not* bald' is also false for the same reason.

Russell started what is sometimes called the 'linguistic turn' in philosophy, a movement in which philosophers began to think very hard about language and its underlying logical form. A.J. Ayer was part of that movement.

CHAPTER 32

Boo!/Hooray!
ALFRED JULES AYER

Wouldn't it be wonderful if you had a way of knowing when someone was talking nonsense? You'd never need to be fooled again. You could divide everything that you heard or read into statements which made sense and statements which were just nonsense and not worth your time. A.J. Ayer (1910–89) believed he'd discovered one. He called it the Verification Principle.

After spending some months in Austria in the early 1930s attending meetings of a group of brilliant scientists and philosophers known as the Vienna Circle, Ayer returned to Oxford where he was working as a lecturer. At the young age of 24 he wrote a book that declared that most of the history of philosophy was filled with gibberish – it was complete nonsense and more or less worthless. That book, published in 1936, was called *Language, Truth and Logic*. It was part of a movement known as logical positivism, a movement that celebrated science as the greatest human achievement.

'Metaphysics' is a word used to describe the study of any reality that lies beyond our senses, the kind of thing that Kant, Schopenhauer and Hegel believed in. For Ayer, though, 'metaphysics' was a dirty word. It was what he was against. Ayer was only interested in what could be known through logic or the senses. But metaphysics often went far beyond either and described realities which couldn't be investigated scientifically or conceptually. As far as Ayer was concerned, that meant it was of no use at all and should be ditched.

Not surprisingly, *Language, Truth and Logic* ruffled feathers. Many of the older philosophers in Oxford hated it, which made it difficult for Ayer to get a job. But ruffling feathers is something philosophers have been doing for thousands of years, in the tradition that began with Socrates. Still, to write a book that so openly attacked the work of some of the great philosophers of the past was a brave thing to do.

Ayer's way of telling meaningful from meaningless sentences was this. Take any sentence, and ask these two questions:

(1) Is it true by definition?
(2) Is it empirically verifiable?

If it was neither of these then it was meaningless. That was his two-pronged test for meaningfulness. Only statements that were true by definition or empirically verifiable were of any use to philosophers. This needs some explanation. Examples of statements that are true by definition are 'All ostriches are birds' or 'All brothers are male'. These are *analytic* statements, in Immanuel Kant's terminology (see Chapter 19). You don't need to go and investigate ostriches to know they are birds – that's part of the definition of an ostrich. And obviously you couldn't have a female brother – no one will ever discover one of those, you can be sure of that; not without a sex change at some point anyway. Statements that are true by definition bring out what is implicit in the terms that we use.

Empirically verifiable statements ('synthetic' statements, in Kant's jargon), in contrast, can give us genuine knowledge. For a statement to be empirically verifiable there has to be some test or observation that will show whether it is true or false. For example if someone says 'All dolphins eat fish' we could get some dolphins and offer them fish and see if they eat some. If we discovered a dolphin that never ate fish, then we'd know that the statement was false. That would still be a verifiable statement for Ayer because he used the word 'verifiable' to cover both 'verifiable' and 'falsifiable'. Empirically verifiable statements were all factual statements: they are about the way the world is. There must be some observation that will support or undermine them. Science is our best way of examining them.

If the sentence was neither true by definition nor empirically verifiable (or falsifiable), then it was, Ayer declared, meaningless. As simple as that. This bit of Ayer's philosophy was borrowed straight from David Hume's work. Hume had half seriously suggested that we should burn works of philosophy that failed this test because they contained nothing but 'sophistry and illusion'. Ayer reworked Hume's ideas for the twentieth century.

So, if we take the sentence 'Some philosophers have beards' then it is fairly obvious that this isn't true by definition, since it isn't part of the definition of a philosopher that some of them must have facial hair. But it is empirically verifiable because it is something we could go out and get evidence about. All we need to do is look at a range of philosophers. If we find some with beards, as we are very likely to do, then we can conclude that the sentence is true. Or, if after looking at many hundreds of philosophers we can't find a single one with a beard, we may conclude that the sentence 'Some philosophers have beards' is probably false, though we can't be sure without examining every philosopher there is. Either way – true or false – the sentence is meaningful.

Compare that with the sentence 'My room is full of invisible angels that leave no trace.' That isn't true by definition either. But is it empirically verifiable? It seems not. There's no imaginable way of detecting these invisible angels if they really leave no trace. You can't touch them or smell them. They don't leave footprints, and they don't make a noise. So the sentence is just nonsense, even though it looks as if it might make sense. It is a grammatically correct sentence, but as a statement about the world, it is neither true nor false. It is meaningless.

This can be quite hard to grasp. The sentence 'My room is full of invisible angels that leave no trace' seems to mean something. But Ayer's point is that it contributes nothing whatsoever to human knowledge, though it might sound poetic or could possibly contribute to a work of fiction.

Ayer didn't just attack metaphysics: ethics and religion were both targets for him too. For example, one of his most challenging conclusions was that moral judgements were literally nonsense. This seemed an outrageous thing to say. But it was what followed if you used his two-pronged test on moral statements. If you say 'Torture is wrong' all you are doing, he thought, was the equivalent of saying 'Torture, boo!' You are revealing your personal emotions about the issue rather than making a statement that could be true or false. That's because 'Torture is wrong' isn't true by definition. Nor is it something that we could ever prove or disprove as a fact. There's no test that you could do that would decide the issue, he believed – something that utilitarians such as Jeremy Bentham and John

Stuart Mill would have disputed, since they would have measured the resulting happiness.

It is therefore, on Ayer's analysis, completely meaningless to say 'Torture is wrong' since it is the type of sentence that could never be either true or false. When you say 'Compassion is good' all you are doing is showing how you feel: it's just like saying 'Compassion, Hooray!' Not surprisingly, Ayer's theory of ethics, known as emotivism, is often described as the Boo!/Hooray! Theory. Some people took Ayer to be saying that morality doesn't matter, that you can choose to do whatever you like. But that wasn't his point. He meant that we couldn't have meaningful discussion of these issues in terms of values, but he did believe that in most debates about what we should do facts were discussed, and these were empirically verifiable.

In another chapter of *Language, Truth and Logic* Ayer attacked the idea that we could talk meaningfully about God. He argued that the statement 'God exists' was neither true nor false; again, it was, he felt, literally meaningless. That's because it wasn't true by definition (though some people, following St Anselm, using the Ontological Argument have said God must necessarily exist). And there wasn't a test you could do to prove God's existence or non-existence – since he rejected the Design Argument. So Ayer was neither a theist (who believes God exists) nor an atheist (who believes that God doesn't exist). Rather he thought that 'God exists' was just another of those meaningless statements – some people give this position the name 'igtheism'. So Ayer was an igtheist, that special category of people who think that all talk of God existing or not existing is complete nonsense.

Despite this, Ayer did get a shock very late in life when he had a near-death experience after choking on a bit of salmon bone and falling unconscious. His heart stopped for four minutes.

During that time he had a clear vision of a red light and two 'Masters of the Universe' talking to each other. This vision didn't make him believe in God, far from it, but it did make him question his certainty about whether the mind could continue existing after death.

Unfortunately for Ayer's logical positivism, it provided the tools for its own destruction. The theory itself didn't seem to pass its own test. First, it's not obvious that the theory is true by definition. Secondly, there is no observation that would prove or disprove it. So by its own standards it is meaningless.

For those who turned to philosophy to help them answer questions about how to live, Ayer's philosophy was of very little use. More promising in many ways was existentialism, the movement that emerged from Europe during and immediately after the Second World War.

CHAPTER 33

The Anguish of Freedom
JEAN-PAUL SARTRE, SIMONE DE BEAUVOIR AND ALBERT CAMUS

If you could travel back in time to 1945 and to a café in Paris called Les Deux Magots ('The Two Wise Men'), you would find yourself sitting near a small man with goggly eyes. He is smoking a pipe and writing in a notebook. This man is Jean-Paul Sartre (1905–80), the most famous existentialist philosopher. He was also a novelist, playwright and biographer. He lived most of his life in hotels and did most of his writing in cafés. He didn't look like a cult figure, but within a few years that's what he would become.

Quite often Sartre would be joined by a beautiful and highly intelligent woman, Simone de Beauvoir (1908–86). They'd known each other since they met at college. She was his long-term companion, though they never married and never lived together. They had other lovers too, but theirs was a long-lasting relationship – they described it as 'essential' and all their other relationships as 'contingent' (meaning 'not necessary'). Like

Sartre, she was a philosopher and a novelist. She wrote an important early feminist book called *The Second Sex* (1949).

During much of the Second World War that had just ended Paris had been occupied by the Nazi forces. Life had been very difficult for the French. Some had managed to join the Resistance fighters and had fought the Germans. Others had collaborated with the Nazis and betrayed their friends to save themselves. Food had been in short supply. There had been gun battles in the streets. People disappeared and were never seen again. The Jews of Paris had been sent to concentration camps, where most were murdered.

Now that the Allies had defeated Germany it was time to start life afresh. There was both relief that the war was over and also a sense that the past had to be left behind. It was time to think through what sort of society there should be. After the terrible things that had happened in the war, all kinds of people were asking themselves the sorts of questions philosophers ask, like 'What is the point of living?', 'Is there a God?', 'Must I always do what others expect me to do?'

Sartre had already written a long and difficult book called *Being and Nothingness* (1943) which was published during the war. The central theme of the book was freedom. Human beings are free. This was an odd message in occupied France when most French people felt like – or really were – prisoners in their own country. What he meant, though, was that, unlike, say, a penknife, a human being wasn't designed to do anything in particular. Sartre didn't believe there was a God who could have designed us, so he rejected the idea that God had a purpose for us. The penknife was designed to cut. That was its essence, what made it what it is. But what was a human being designed to do? Human beings don't have an essence. We aren't here for a reason, he thought. There is no particular way we have to be to be human. A human being can choose what to do, what to become. We are all free. No one but you can decide what you make of your life. If you let other people decide how you live, that is, again, a choice. It would be a choice to be the kind of person other people expect you to be.

Obviously if you make a choice to do something, you might not always succeed in doing it. And the reasons why you don't succeed may be completely outside your control. But you are responsible for wanting to do that thing, for trying to do it, and for how you respond to your failure to be able to do it.

Freedom is hard to handle and many of us run away from it. One of the ways to hide is to pretend that you aren't really free at all. If Sartre is right, we can't make excuses: we are completely responsible for what we do every day and how we feel about what we do. Right down to the emotions we have. If you're sad right now, that's your choice, according to Sartre. You don't have to be sad. If you are sad, you are responsible for it. That is frightening and some people would rather not face up to it because it is so painful. He talks about us being 'condemned to be free'. We're stuck with this freedom whether we like it or not.

Sartre described a waiter in a café. This café waiter moves in a very stylized way, acting as if he is a kind of puppet. Everything about him suggests that he thinks of himself as completely defined by his role as a waiter, as if he has no choice about anything. The way he holds the tray, the way he moves between the tables, are all part of a kind of dance – a dance that is choreographed by his job as a waiter, not by the human being performing it. Sartre says this man is in 'bad faith'. Bad faith is running away from freedom. It is a kind of lie you tell yourself and almost believe: the lie that you aren't really free to choose what to do with your life, when, according to Sartre, whether you like it or not, you are.

In a lecture he gave just after the war, 'Existentialism is a Humanism', Sartre described human life as full of anguish. The anguish comes from understanding that we can't make any excuses but are responsible for everything we do. But the anguish is worse because, according to Sartre, whatever I do with my life is a kind of template for what anyone else should do with their life. If I decide to marry, I'm suggesting that everyone should marry; if I decide to be lazy, that's what everyone should do in my vision of human existence. Through the choices I make in my life I paint a picture of what I think a human being ought to be like. If I do this sincerely it is a great responsibility.

Sartre explained what he meant by the anguish of choice through the true story of a student who had come to ask his advice during the war. This young man had to make a very difficult decision. He could either stay at home to look after his mother; or he could run off and try to join the French Resistance and fight to save his country from the Germans. This was the most difficult decision of his life and he wasn't sure what to do. If he left his mother, she would be vulnerable without him. He might not succeed in getting to the Resistance fighters before being caught by the Germans, and then the whole attempt to do something noble would be a waste of energy and of a life. But if he stayed at home with his mother, he'd be letting others do the fighting for him. What should he do? What would you do? What advice would you give him?

Sartre's advice was a bit frustrating. He told the student that he was free and that he should choose for himself. If Sartre had given the student any practical advice about what to do, the student would still have had to decide whether or not to follow it. There is no way to escape the weight of responsibility that comes with being human.

'Existentialism' was the name that other people gave to Sartre's philosophy. The name came from the idea that we find ourselves first of all *existing* in the world, and then have to decide what we will make of our lives. It could have been the other way round: we could have been like a penknife, designed for a particular purpose. But, Sartre believed, we aren't. In his way of putting it, our existence comes before our essence, whereas for designed objects their essence comes before their existence.

In *The Second Sex*, Simone de Beauvoir gave this existentialism a different twist by claiming that women are not born women; they become women. What she meant was that women tend to accept men's view of what a woman is. To be what men expect you to be is a choice. But women, being free, can decide for themselves what they want to be. They have no essence, no way given by nature that they have to be.

Another important theme of existentialism was the absurdity of our existence. Life doesn't have any meaning at all until we give it meaning by making choices, and then before too long death comes and removes all the meaning that we can give it. Sartre's version of this was to describe a human being as 'a useless passion': there is no point to our existence at all. There is only the meaning each of us creates through our choices. Albert Camus (1913–60), a novelist and philosopher also linked with existentialism, used the Greek myth of Sisyphus to explain human absurdity. Sisyphus' punishment for tricking the gods is that he has to roll a huge rock to the top of a mountain. When he reaches the top, the rock rolls down and he has to begin from the bottom once more. Sisyphus has to do this again and again for ever. Human life is like Sisyphus' task in that it is completely meaningless. There is no point to it: no answers that will explain everything. It's absurd. But Camus didn't think we should despair. We shouldn't commit suicide. Instead we have to recognize that Sisyphus is happy. Why is he happy? Because there is something about the pointless struggle of rolling that huge rock up the mountain that makes his life worth living. It is still preferable to death.

Existentialism became a cult. Thousands of young people were drawn to it and would discuss the absurdity of human existence late into the night. It inspired novels, plays and films. It was a philosophy that people could live by and apply to their own decisions. Sartre himself became more politically involved and more left wing as he got older, and he tried to combine the insights of Marxism with his earlier ideas – a difficult task. His existentialism of the 1940s focused on individuals making choices for themselves; but in his later work he tried to make sense of how we are part of a larger group of people and how social and economic factors play a role in our lives. Unfortunately his writing got more and more difficult to understand, perhaps in part because much of it was written while he was high on amphetamines.

Sartre was probably the best-known philosopher of the twentieth century. But if you ask philosophers who was the most important thinker of the last century, many of them will tell you that it was Ludwig Wittgenstein.

CHAPTER 34

Bewitched by Language
Ludwig Wittgenstein

If you found yourself at one of the seminars Ludwig Wittgenstein (1889–1951) held in Cambridge in 1940 you would very quickly realize that you were in the presence of someone very unusual. Most people who met him thought he was a genius. Bertrand Russell described him as 'passionate, profound, intense and dominating'. This small Viennese man with bright blue eyes and a deep seriousness about him would pace up and down, asking students questions, or pause lost in thought for minutes at a time. No one dared interrupt. He didn't lecture from prepared notes, but thought through the issues in front of his audience, using a series of examples to tease out what was at stake. He told his students not to waste their time reading philosophy books; if they took such books seriously, he said, they should throw them across the room and get on with thinking hard about the puzzles they raised.

His own first book, the *Tractatus Logico-Philosophicus* (1922), was written in numbered short sections, many of which read more like poetry than philosophy. Its main message was that the most important questions about ethics and religion lie beyond the limits of our understanding and that if we can't talk meaningfully about them, we should stay silent.

A central theme in this later work was 'bewitchment by language'. Language leads philosophers into all sorts of confusion, he believed. They fall under its spell. Wittgenstein saw his role as that of a therapist who would make much of this confusion go away. The idea was that you would follow the logic of his various carefully chosen examples and that as you did this your philosophical problems would vanish. What had seemed terribly important would no longer be a problem.

One cause of philosophical confusion was, he suggested, the assumption that all language works in the same way – the idea that words simply name things. He wanted to demonstrate to his readers that there are many 'language games', different activities that we perform using words. There is no 'essence' of language, no single common feature that explains the whole range of its uses.

If you see a group of people who are related to each other, at a wedding for example, you may be able to recognize members of the family from physical resemblances between them. That is what Wittgenstein meant by a 'family resemblance'. So you may look a bit like your mother in some ways – perhaps you both have the same hair and eye colour – and a bit like your grandfather in that you are both tall and slim. You might also have the same hair colour and eye shape as your sister, but she might have different-coloured eyes from you and your mother. There is not one single feature that every member of the family shares that makes it straightforward to see that you are all part of the same genetically related family. Instead, there is a pattern of overlapping resemblances, with some of you sharing some features, and others sharing different features. That pattern of overlapping resemblances is what interested Wittgenstein. He used this metaphor of family resemblance to explain something important about how language works.

Think about the word 'game'. There are lots of different things that we call games: board games like chess, card games like bridge and patience, sports like football, and so on. There are also other things that we call games, such as games of hide-and-seek or games of make-believe. Most people just assume that because we use the same word – 'game' – to cover all these, there must be a single feature that they all have in common, the 'essence' of the concept 'game'. But rather than just assuming that there is such a common denominator, Wittgenstein urges his readers to 'Look and see'. You might think that games all have a winner and a loser, but what about solitaire, or the activity of throwing a ball at a wall and catching it? Both of these are games, but obviously there isn't a loser. Or what about the idea that what they have in common is a set of rules? But some games of make-believe don't seem to have rules. For every candidate for a common feature of all games, Wittgenstein comes up with a counter-example, a case of something that is a game but that doesn't seem to share the suggested 'essence' of all games. Instead of assuming that all games have a single thing in common, he thinks we should see words like 'game' as 'family resemblance terms'.

When Wittgenstein described language as a series of 'language games' he was drawing attention to the fact that there are many different things that we use language for, and that philosophers have become confused because they mostly think that all language is doing the same sort of thing. In one of his famous descriptions of his aim as a philosopher, he said that what he wanted to do was show the fly the way out of the fly bottle. A typical philosopher will buzz around like a fly trapped in a bottle, banging against the sides. The way to 'solve' a philosophical problem was to remove the cork and let the fly out. What this meant was that he wanted to show the philosopher that he or she had been asking the wrong questions or had been misled by language.

Take St Augustine's description of how he had learnt to speak. In his *Confessions*, he suggested that the older people around him would point to objects and name them. He sees an apple, someone points to it and says 'apple'. Gradually Augustine understood what the words meant and was able to use them to tell other people what he wanted. Wittgenstein took this account to be a case of someone assuming that all language had an essence, a single function. The single function was to name objects. For Augustine, every word has a meaning that it stands for. In place of this picture of language, Wittgenstein encourages us to see language use as a series of activities that are tied up with the practical lives of speakers. We should think of language as more like a tool bag containing many different sorts of tools, rather than as, for example, always serving the function that a screwdriver does.

It may seem obvious to you that when you are in pain and you speak about it what you are doing is using words which name the particular sensation you have. But Wittgenstein tries to disrupt that view of the language of sensation. It's not that you don't have a sensation. It's just that, logically, your words can't be the names of sensations. If everybody had a box with a beetle in that they never showed to anyone, it wouldn't really matter what was in the box when they talked to one another about their 'beetle'. Language is public, and it requires publicly available ways of checking that we are making sense. When a child learns to 'describe' her pain, Wittgenstein says, what happens is that the parent encourages the child to do various things, such as say 'It hurts' – the equivalent in many ways to the quite natural expression 'Aaargh!' Part of his message here is that we should not think of the words 'I am in pain' as a way of naming a private sensation. If pains and other sensations really were private we would need a special private language to describe them. But Wittgenstein thought that idea didn't make sense. Another of his examples may help explain why he thought this.

A man decides that he will keep a record of every time he has a particular kind of sensation for which there is no name – perhaps a specific kind of tingle. He writes 'S' in his diary whenever he feels that special tingling sensation. 'S' is a word in his private language – no one else knows what he means by it. This sounds as if it is possible. It isn't difficult to imagine a man doing exactly this. But then, think a bit harder. How does he know when he gets a tingle that it really is a further example of the type 'S' he's decided to record and not another kind of tingle? He can't go back and check it against anything except his memory of having an earlier 'S' tingling experience. That's not really good enough, though, because he could be completely mistaken about it. It isn't a reliable way of telling that you are using the word in the same way.

The point he was trying to make with his example of the diary was that the way we use words to describe our experiences can't be based on a private linking of the experience with the word. There must be something public about it. We can't have our own private language. And if that is true, the idea that the mind is like a locked theatre that no one else can get into is misleading. For Wittgenstein, then, the idea of a private language of sensations doesn't make sense at all. This is important – and difficult to grasp too – because many philosophers before him thought that each individual's mind was completely private.

Although Christian by religion, the Wittgenstein family was considered Jewish under Nazi laws. Ludwig spent part of the Second World War working as an orderly in a London hospital, but his extended family were lucky to escape from Vienna. Had they not, Adolf Eichmann might have overseen their deportation to the death camps. Eichmann's involvement in the Holocaust and his later trial for crimes against humanity were the focus of Hannah Arendt's reflections on the nature of evil.

CHAPTER 35

The Man Who Didn't Ask Questions
Hannah Arendt

The Nazi Adolf Eichmann was a hard-working administrator. From 1942 he was in charge of transporting the Jews of Europe to concentration camps in Poland, including Auschwitz. This was part of Adolf Hitler's 'Final Solution': his plan to kill all Jews living in land occupied by the German forces. Eichmann wasn't responsible for the policy of systematic killing – it was not his idea. But he was heavily involved in organizing the railway system that made it possible.

Since the 1930s the Nazis had been introducing laws that took away the rights of Jewish people. Hitler blamed almost everything that was wrong with Germany on the Jews and had a mad wish to get revenge on them. These laws prevented Jews from going to state-run schools, forced them to hand over money and property, and made them wear a yellow star. Jews were rounded up and forced to live in ghettos – overcrowded sections of cities that became prisons for them. Food was scarce, and life was difficult. But the Final Solution introduced a new level of evil. Hitler's decision to murder millions of people simply because of their race meant that the Nazis needed a way of getting the Jews out of the cities to places where they could be killed in large numbers. Existing concentration camps were turned into factories for gassing and cremating hundreds of people a day. As many of these camps were in Poland, someone had to organize the trains that transported the Jews to their deaths.

While Eichmann sat shuffling bits of paper in an office and making important telephone calls, millions died as a result of what he did. Some perished from typhoid or starvation, others were made to work until they died, but most were killed with gas. In Nazi Germany the trains ran on time – Eichmann and people like him made sure of that. Their efficiency kept the cattle trucks full. Inside were men, women and children, all on a long and painful journey to their death, usually without food or water, sometimes in intense heat or cold. Many died on the journey, particularly the old and sick.

The survivors arrived weak and terrified, only to be forced into chambers disguised as shower rooms where they were made to strip naked. The doors were locked. It was here that the Nazis murdered them with Zyklon gas. Their bodies were burned and their possessions plundered. If they weren't selected for immediate death in this way, the stronger ones among them might be forced to work in atrocious conditions with little food. The Nazi guards would beat or even shoot them for fun.

Eichmann played a significant role in these crimes. Yet after the Second World War ended he managed to escape from the Allies, eventually arriving in Argentina, where he lived for some years in secret. In 1960, though, members of the Israeli secret police, Mossad, tracked him down to Buenos Aires and captured him. They drugged him and flew him back to Israel to stand trial.

Was Eichmann some kind of evil beast, a sadist who enjoyed other people's suffering? That was what most people believed before the trial began. How else could he have played this part in the Holocaust? For several years his job was to find efficient ways to send people to their death. Surely only a monster would be capable of sleeping at night after that kind of work.

The philosopher Hannah Arendt (1906–75), a German Jew who had emigrated to the United States, reported on Eichmann's trial for the *New Yorker* magazine. She was interested in coming face to face with a product of the Nazi totalitarian state, a society in which there was little room to think for yourself. She wanted to understand this man, get a sense of what he was like; and see how he could have done such terrible things.

Eichmann was very far from the first Nazi that Arendt had met. She fled the Nazis herself, leaving Germany for France, but eventually becoming a US citizen. As a young woman at the University of Marburg her teacher had been the philosopher Martin Heidegger. For a short while they were lovers even though she was only 18 and he was married. Heidegger was busy writing *Being and Time*, an incredibly difficult book that some people think is a major contribution to philosophy and others a deliberately obscure piece of writing. Later he would become a committed member of the Nazi Party, supporting its anti-Jewish policies. He even removed the name of his former friend, the philosopher Edmund Husserl, from the dedication page of *Being and Time* because he was Jewish.

But now in Jerusalem, Arendt was to meet a very different sort of Nazi. Here was a rather ordinary man who chose not to think too hard about what he was doing. His failure to think had disastrous consequences. But he wasn't the evil sadist that she might have expected to find. He was something far more common but equally dangerous: an unthinking man. In a Germany where the worst forms of racism had been written into the law, it was easy for him to persuade himself that what he was doing was right. Circumstances gave him the opportunity for a successful career, and he took it. Hitler's Final Solution was an opportunity for Eichmann to do well, to show that he could do a good job. This is difficult to imagine, and many critics of Arendt don't think she was right, but she felt that he was sincere when he claimed to be doing his duty.

Unlike some Nazis, Eichmann didn't seem to be driven by a strong hatred of Jews. He had none of Hitler's venom. There were plenty of Nazis who would have happily beaten a Jew to death in the street for failing to give the 'Heil Hitler!' greeting, but he wasn't one of them. Yet he had taken on the official Nazi line and had accepted it, but far, far worse than that, he had helped send millions to their death. Even as he listened to the evidence against him he seemed to see little wrong with what he had done. As far as he was concerned, since he had not broken any laws, and had never directly killed anyone himself or asked anyone else to do that for him, he had behaved reasonably. He had been brought up to obey the law and trained to follow orders, and all around him people were doing the same as he was. By taking commands from other people he avoided feeling responsible for the results of his daily work.

There was no need for Eichmann to see people bundled into cattle trucks or to visit the death camps, so he didn't. This was a man who told the court he couldn't have become a doctor because he was afraid of the sight of blood. Yet the blood was still on his hands. He was a product of a system that had somehow prevented him thinking critically about his own actions and the results they produced for real people. It was as if he couldn't imagine other people's feelings at all. He carried on with his deluded belief in his innocence all through his trial. Either that, or he had decided that his best line of defence was to say he was only obeying the law; if so, he took Arendt in.

Arendt used the words 'the banality of evil' to describe what she saw in Eichmann. If something is 'banal', it is common, boring and unoriginal. Eichmann's evil was, she claimed, banal in the sense that it was the evil of a bureaucrat, of an office manager, rather than a devil. Here was this very ordinary sort of man who had allowed Nazi views to affect everything he did.

Arendt's philosophy was inspired by events around her. She wasn't the kind of philosopher to spend her life in an armchair thinking about purely abstract ideas or debating endlessly about the precise meaning of a word. Her philosophy was linked to recent history and lived experience. What she wrote in her book *Eichmann in Jerusalem* was based on her observations of one man and the sorts of language and justifications he gave. From what she saw she developed more general explanations of evil in a totalitarian state and its effects on those who did not resist its thought patterns.

Eichmann, like many Nazis during that era, failed to see things from someone else's perspective. He wasn't brave enough to question the rules that he was given: he simply looked for the best way to follow them. He lacked imagination. Arendt described him as shallow and brainless – though that too could have been an act. Had he been a monster he would have been terrifying. But at least monsters are rare and usually quite easy to spot. What was perhaps more terrifying still was the fact that he appeared so normal. He was an ordinary man who, by failing to question what he was doing, took part in some of the most evil acts known to humanity. If he had not lived in Nazi Germany it is unlikely that he would have been an evil man. Circumstances were against him. But that doesn't remove his guilt. He was obedient to immoral orders. And obeying Nazi orders was, as far as Arendt was concerned, the same as supporting the Final Solution. By failing to question what he was told to do, and by carrying out those orders, he took part in mass murder even though from his point of view he was just creating train timetables. At one point in his trial he even claimed to be acting according to Immanuel Kant's theory of moral duty – as if he had done the right thing by following orders. He completely failed to understand that Kant believed that treating human beings with respect and dignity was fundamental to morality.

Karl Popper was a Viennese intellectual fortunate enough to escape the Holocaust and Eichmann's well-timetabled trains.

CHAPTER 36

Learning from Mistakes
KARL POPPER AND THOMAS KUHN

In 1666 a young scientist was sitting in a garden when an apple fell to the ground. This made him wonder why apples fall straight down, rather than going off to the side or upwards. The scientist was Isaac Newton, and the incident inspired him to come up with his theory of gravity, a theory that explained the movements of planets as well as apples. But what happened next? Do you think that Newton then gathered evidence that *proved* beyond all doubt that his theory was true? Not according to Karl Popper (1902–94).

Scientists, like all of us, learn from their mistakes. Science progresses when we realize that a particular way of thinking about reality is false. That, in two sentences, was Karl Popper's view of how humanity's best hope for knowledge about the world functions. Before he developed his ideas most people believed that scientists begin with a hunch about how the world is, and then gather evidence that shows their hunch was correct.

What scientists do, according to Popper, is try to prove their theories are *false*. Testing a theory involves seeing if it can be *refuted* (shown to be false). A typical scientist starts with a bold guess or conjecture that he or she then tries to undermine in a series of experiments or observations. Science is a creative and exciting enterprise, but it doesn't prove anything is true – all it does is get rid of false views and – hopefully – edge towards truth in the process.

Popper was born in Vienna in 1902. Although his family had converted to Christianity, he was descended from Jews and when Hitler came to power in the 1930s Popper wisely left the country, moving first to New Zealand, and later to England where he settled, and took up a post at the London School of Economics. As a young man he had wide-ranging interests in science, psychology, politics and music, but philosophy was his real love. By the end of his life he had made important contributions both to the philosophy of science and to political philosophy.

Until Popper started writing about scientific method, many scientists and philosophers believed that the way to do science was to seek out evidence that supported your hypothesis. If you wanted to prove that all swans are white you'd make a lot of observations of white swans. If all the swans you looked at were white, it seemed reasonable to assume that your hypothesis 'All swans are white' was true. This style of reasoning goes from 'All the swans I've seen are white' to the conclusion 'All swans are white.' But clearly a swan that you haven't observed could turn out to be black. There are black swans in Australia, for example, and in many zoos around the world. So the statement 'All swans are white' doesn't follow logically from the evidence. Even if you have looked at thousands of swans and they were all white, it could still be false. The only way to prove conclusively that they are all white is to look at every single swan. If just one black swan exists, your conclusion 'All swans are white' will have been falsified.

This is a version of the Problem of Induction, a problem that David Hume wrote about in the eighteenth century. Induction is very different from deduction. That is the source of the problem. Deduction is a type of logical argument where if the premises (the starting assumptions) are true the conclusion must be true. So, to take a famous example, 'All men are mortal' and 'Socrates is a man' are two premises from which the logical conclusion 'Socrates is mortal' follows. You would contradict yourself if you agreed that 'All men are mortal' *and* that 'Socrates is a man', but denied the truth of the statement 'Socrates is mortal.' That would be like saying 'Socrates both is and is not mortal.' One way of thinking about this is that with deduction the truth of the conclusion is somehow contained within the premises and logic just teases it out. Here's another example of deduction:

Premise one: All fish have gills.
Premise two: John is a fish.
Conclusion: Therefore John has gills.

It would be absurd to say that premise one and premise two were true, but that the conclusion was false. That would be completely illogical.

Induction is very different from this. Induction usually involves arguing from a selection of observations to a general conclusion. If you notice that it rained every Tuesday for four consecutive weeks, you might generalize from this that it always rains on Tuesdays. That would be a case of Induction. It would only take one dry Tuesday to undermine the claim that it always rains on Tuesdays. Four consecutive wet Tuesdays is a small sample of all the possible Tuesdays. But even if you make numerous observations, as with the white swans, you can still be thwarted by the existence of a single case that doesn't fit your generalization: one dry Tuesday or one non-white swan, for example. And that is the Problem of Induction, the problem of justifying relying on the method of induction when it seems so unreliable. How do you know that the next glass of water you drink won't poison you? Answer: all the glasses of water you've drunk in the past were fine. So you assume that this one will be. We use this kind of reasoning all the time. Yet it seems that we aren't completely justified in putting such faith in it. We assume patterns in nature that may or may not really be there.

If you think that science progresses by induction, as many philosophers have done, then you have to face the Problem of Induction. How can science be based on such an unreliable style of reasoning? Popper's view of how science develops neatly avoids this problem. That's because, according to him, science doesn't rely on induction. Scientists start with a hypothesis, an informed guess about the nature of reality. An example might be 'All gases expand when heated.' This is a simple hypothesis, but real-life science involves a great deal of creativity and imagination at this stage. Scientists find their ideas in many places: the chemist August Kekulé, for example, famously dreamt of a snake biting its own tail, which gave him the idea for the hypothesis that the structure of the benzene molecule is a hexagonal ring – a hypothesis that has so far stood up to scientists' attempts to prove it false.

Scientists then find a way of testing this hypothesis – in this case, getting a lot of different sorts of gas and heating them. But 'testing' doesn't mean finding evidence to *support* the hypothesis; it means trying to prove that the hypothesis can survive attempts to *falsify* it. Ideally the scientists will look for a gas that doesn't fit the hypothesis. Remember that in the case of the swans it only took one black swan to undermine the generalization that all swans are white. Similarly, it would only take one gas that failed to expand when heated to undermine the hypothesis that 'All gases expand when heated.'

If a scientist refutes a hypothesis – that is, shows that it is false – then that results in a new bit of knowledge: the knowledge that the hypothesis is false. Humanity progresses because we learn something. Observing lots of gases which *do* expand when heated won't give us knowledge, except perhaps a little more confidence in our hypothesis. But a counter-example really teaches us something. For Popper a key feature of any hypothesis is that it has to be *falsifiable*. He used this idea to explain the difference between science and what he called 'pseudo-science'. A scientific hypothesis is one that can be proved wrong: it makes predictions that can be shown to be false. If I say 'There are invisible, undetectable fairies making me type this sentence', then there is no observation that you can make that will prove my statement is false. If the fairies are invisible and don't leave any trace, there is no way of showing that the claim that they exist is false. It is unfalsifiable and so not a scientific statement at all.

Popper thought that many statements made about psychoanalysis (see Chapter 30) were unfalsifiable in this way. He thought they were untestable. For example, if someone says that everyone is motivated by unconscious wishes, there is no test to prove this. Every bit of evidence, including people denying that they are motivated by unconscious wishes, is, according to Popper, merely taken as further proof that psychoanalysis is valid. The psychoanalyst will say, 'The fact that you deny the unconscious demonstrates that you have a strong unconscious wish to challenge your father.' But this statement can't be tested because there is no imaginable evidence that could show that it was false. Consequently, Popper argued, psychoanalysis wasn't a science. It couldn't give us knowledge in the way a science could. Popper attacked Marxist accounts of history in the same way, arguing that every possible outcome would count as support for the view that the history of humanity is a history of class struggle. So again, it was based on unfalsifiable hypotheses.

In contrast, Albert Einstein's theory that light would be attracted by the sun *was* falsifiable. That made it a scientific theory. In 1919 observations of the apparent position of stars during an eclipse of the sun failed to refute it. But they might have done. The light from the stars was not normally visible, but under the rare conditions of an eclipse scientists were able to see that the stars' apparent positions were where Einstein's theory predicted they would be. If they had seemed to be somewhere else, this would have undermined Einstein's theory of how light is attracted to very heavy bodies. Popper didn't think these observations proved that Einstein's theory was true. But the testability of the theory, and the fact that scientists had been unable to show it to be false, counted in its favour. Einstein made predictions which could have been wrong, but they weren't.

Many scientists and philosophers have been deeply impressed by Popper's description of scientific method. Peter Medawar, who won the Nobel Prize for Medicine, for example, said, 'I think Karl Popper is incomparably the greatest philosopher of science there has ever been.' The scientists particularly liked the description of their activity as creative and imaginative; they also felt that Popper understood how they actually went about their work. The philosophers were delighted with the way that

Popper got around the difficult issue of the Problem of Induction too. In 1962, however, the American historian of science and physicist Thomas Kuhn published a book called *The Structure of Scientific Revolutions*, which told a different story of how science progresses, one that suggested Popper had got things wrong. Kuhn believed that Popper hadn't looked closely enough at the history of science. If he had he would have seen a pattern emerging.

Most of the time what he called 'normal science' goes on. Scientists work within a framework or 'paradigm' that the scientists of that day share. So, for example, before people realized that the earth revolves around the sun, the paradigm was that the sun goes round the earth. Astronomers would do their research within that framework and would have explanations of any evidence that didn't seem to fit with it. Working within this paradigm, a scientist like Copernicus who came up with the idea that the earth goes round the sun would be thought to have made a mistake in his calculations. According to Kuhn, there aren't facts out there waiting to be discovered: instead, the framework or paradigm to some extent fixes what you can think about.

Things get interesting when what Kuhn called a 'paradigm shift' happens. A paradigm shift is when a whole way of understanding is overturned. This can happen when scientists find things that don't fit in with the existing paradigm – such as observations that didn't make sense within the paradigm that the sun goes round the earth. But even then it can take a long time for people to abandon their old ways of thinking. Scientists who have spent their lives working within one paradigm don't usually welcome a different way of looking at the world. When they do eventually switch to a new paradigm, a period of normal science can begin again, this time working within the new framework. And so it goes on. That's what happened when the view that the earth was the centre of the universe was overturned. Once people started to think about the solar system in that way, there was a lot more normal science to do to understand the paths of the planets around the sun.

Popper, not surprisingly, didn't agree with this account of the history of science, although he did agree that the concept of 'normal science' was useful. Whether he was like a scientist with an outdated paradigm himself, or had got closer to the truth about reality than Kuhn had, is an intriguing question.

Scientists use real experiments; philosophers, on the other hand, tend to invent thought experiments to make their arguments plausible. The philosophers Philippa Foot and Judith Jarvis Thomson have developed a number of carefully constructed thought experiments that reveal important features of our moral thinking.

CHAPTER 37

The Runaway Train and the Unwanted Violinist

Philippa Foot and Judith Jarvis Thomson

You are out for a walk one day and see a runaway train hurtling down the tracks towards five workers. The driver is unconscious, possibly as the result of a heart attack. If nothing is done, all will die. The train will squash them. It's travelling much too fast for them to get out of the way. There is, however, one hope. There is a fork in the tracks just before the five men, and on the other line there is only one worker. You are close enough to the points to flick the switch and make the train veer away from the five and kill the single worker. Is killing this innocent man the right thing to do? In terms of numbers it clearly is: you save five people by killing just one. That must maximize happiness. To most people this seems the right thing to do. In real life it would be very difficult to flick that switch and watch someone die as a result, but it would be even worse to hold back and watch five times as many people die.

This is a version of a thought experiment originally created by the British philosopher Philippa Foot (1920–2010). She was interested in why saving the five people on the track was acceptable, but some other cases of sacrificing one to save many weren't. Imagine a healthy person walking into a hospital ward. In the ward are five people who desperately need various organs. If one doesn't get a heart transplant she will certainly die. Another needs a liver, one a kidney, and so on. Would it be acceptable to kill the healthy patient and slice up the body to provide the organs for the unhealthy ones? Hardly. No one believes that it would be acceptable to kill the one healthy person, remove his heart, lungs, liver, kidneys, and implant them in the five. Yet that is a case of sacrificing one to save five. What's the difference between that and the runaway train?

A thought experiment is an imaginary situation designed to bring out our feelings, or what philosophers call 'intuitions', on a particular issue. Philosophers use them a lot. Thought experiments allow us to focus more closely on what is at stake. Here the philosophical question is, 'When is it acceptable to sacrifice one life to save more?' The story about the runaway carriage allows us to think about this. It isolates the key factors and shows us whether or not we feel that such an action is wrong.

Some people say you should never flick the switch in this example because that would be 'playing God': deciding who should die and who should live. Most people, however, think you should.

But imagine a related case. The American philosopher Judith Jarvis Thomson thought up this version of the original problem. The runaway train this time is on a straight piece of track running towards the five unfortunate workers who will certainly be killed unless you do something. You are standing on a bridge, and next to you is a very large man. If you push him over the bridge, he is heavy enough to slow down and stop the train before it hits the five workers. Assuming you have the strength to push this man over in front of the train, should you do it?

Many people find this a tougher case, and are more inclined to say 'no', despite the fact that in both this case and in the case of the fork in the line and the points that you can switch the consequence of your actions is the death of one person rather than five. In fact, pushing the large man off the bridge looks very like murder. If the consequences are the same in the two cases then there shouldn't be an issue. If it is right to flick the switch in the first example, it must surely be right to push the large man in front of the train in the second. This is puzzling.

If the imaginary situation of pushing someone over a bridge suggests physical difficulties, or you are put off by the brutality of having to wrestle the man to his death, the case can be revised so that there is a trapdoor on the bridge. Using the same kind of lever as you do in the first case with the point-switching, you can drop the large man into the path of the train with minimal effort. You just flick a lever. Many people see this as morally far removed from the fork in the line case. Why should this be so?

The so-called Law of Double Effect is one explanation of why we think the forking track case and the fat man case are different. This is the belief that it can be all right, for example, to hit someone so hard that they die but only if your intention is to defend yourself and a lighter blow wouldn't protect you. Predictable bad side effects of an action with a good intention (in this case saving yourself) can be acceptable, but deliberate harm is not. It isn't right to go out and poison someone who is planning to kill you. The first case is one in which you have an acceptable intention, it's just that following through on it will result in someone's death. In the second case you intend to kill the person, and that isn't acceptable. For some people, this solves the problem. Other people think this principle of Double Effect is a mistake.

These cases may seem far-fetched and nothing to do with everyday life. In one sense that is true. They're not meant to be real cases. These are thought experiments designed to clarify our beliefs. But from time to time real-life situations do arise that lead to similar decisions. For example, during the Second World War the Nazis were firing flying bombs into parts of London. A German spy had become a double agent. The British had the chance to send misleading information back to the Germans, telling them that the rockets were falling far to the north of their intended targets. This would have had the effect of making the Germans change their aim, so that instead of falling on heavily populated parts of London, the rockets would fall further to the south on people in Kent and Surrey. In other words, there was a possibility of giving information that would cause fewer people to be killed. In this case the British decided not to play God.

In a different sort of real-life situation, the participants *did* decide to take action. In the Zeebrugge disaster in 1987, when a car ferry sank and dozens of passengers were struggling to get out of the icy sea, a young man climbing to safety on a rope ladder froze with fear and could not move. He stayed in that position for at least ten minutes, stopping anyone else from getting out of the sea. If they didn't get out quickly they would drown or die of cold. Eventually those in the water pulled him off the ladder and managed to escape to safety. The young man fell into the sea and drowned. The decision to pull the young man off the ladder must have been an agonizing one to make, but in these extreme circumstances, as with the runaway train, sacrificing one person to save many was probably the right thing to do.

Philosophers are still arguing about the train example and how it should be solved. They're also arguing about another thought experiment that Judith Jarvis Thomson (born 1929) came up with. This one was to show that a woman who had used contraception but who had still become pregnant did not have a moral duty to go through with having the baby. She could have an abortion without doing something morally wrong. To have the baby in such circumstances would be an act of charity, but not a duty. Traditionally, debates about the morality of abortion had focused on the foetus' point of view. Her argument was important in that it gave a lot of weight to the woman's perspective. Here's the example.

There is a famous violinist who has a kidney problem. His only chance of survival is to be plugged into a person who shares his very rare blood group. You have that same blood group. One morning you wake up to find that while you were asleep doctors have attached him to your kidneys. Thomson argues that in such a situation you don't have a duty to keep him plugged into you, even though you know that he will die if you pull the tubes out. In the same way, she suggests, if a woman is pregnant even though she used contraception, the developing foetus inside her does not have an automatic right to the use of her body. The foetus is like the violinist.

Before Thomson introduced this example, many people thought that the crucial question was, 'Is a foetus a person?' They believed that if they could show that a foetus *was* a person, then abortion would obviously be immoral in every case. Thomson's thought experiment suggested that even if the foetus is a person, that doesn't settle the question.

Of course, not everyone agrees with this answer. Some people still think that you shouldn't play God even if you wake up with a violinist plugged into your kidneys. It would be a difficult life, unless you really loved violin music. But it would still be wrong to kill the violinist even though you had not chosen to help him. Likewise, plenty of people believe that you should never deliberately terminate a healthy pregnancy even if you did not intend to get pregnant and took precautions against doing so. What the cleverly constructed thought experiment does, though, is bring out the principles underlying these disagreements.

The political philosopher John Rawls also used a thought experiment, in his case to investigate the nature of justice and the best principles for organizing society.

CHAPTER 38

Fairness through Ignorance
John Rawls

Perhaps you're wealthy. Perhaps you're super-rich. But most of us aren't, and some people are very poor, so poor that they spend most of their short lives hungry and sick. This doesn't seem fair or right – and it surely isn't. If there were true justice in the world no children would starve while others have so much money that they don't know what to do with it. Everyone who is sick would have access to good medical treatment. The poor of Africa wouldn't be so much worse off than the poor in the USA and Britain. The rich of the West wouldn't be so many thousand times as rich as those who through no fault of their own were born into disadvantage. Justice is about treating people fairly. There are people around us whose lives are filled with good things, and others who, through no fault of their own, get few choices about how they survive: they can't choose the job they do, or even the town where they live. Some people who think about these inequalities will just say, 'Oh well, life's not fair' and shrug their shoulders. These are usually the ones who have been particularly lucky; others will spend time thinking about how society could be better organized and perhaps try to change it to make it fairer.

John Rawls (1921–2002), a modest, quiet Harvard academic, wrote a book that changed the way people thought about these things. That book was *A Theory of Justice* (1971) and the result of nearly twenty years of hard thinking. It's really a professor's book meant for other professors and written in a rather dry academic style. Unlike most books of this kind, though, it didn't sit gathering dust in a library – far from it. It became a bestseller. In some ways it's amazing that so many people read it. But its key ideas were so interesting that it was very quickly declared one of the most influential books of the twentieth century, read by philosophers, lawyers, politicians and many others – something Rawls himself had never dreamt was possible.

Rawls had fought in the Second World War, and was in the Pacific on 6 August 1945 when the atom bomb was dropped on the Japanese city of Hiroshima. He was deeply affected by his wartime experiences and believed that it had been wrong to use nuclear weapons. Like many who lived through that period, he wanted to create a better world, a better society. But his way of bringing about change was through thinking and writing, rather than joining political causes and rallies. While he was writing *A Theory of Justice*, the Vietnam war was raging, and across the United States large-scale anti-war protests – not all of them peaceful – were taking place. Rawls chose to write about abstract general questions of justice rather than getting caught up in the issues of the moment. At the heart of his work was the idea that we need to think clearly about how we live together and the ways in which the state influences our lives. For our existence to be bearable we need to co-operate. But how?

Imagine you have to design a new and better society. One question you might ask is, 'Who gets what?' If you live in a beautiful mansion with an indoor swimming pool and servants, and have a private jet waiting to whisk you away to a tropical island, you might well conjure up a world in which some people are very rich – perhaps the ones who work hardest – and others much poorer. If you are living in poverty now, you'll probably design a society in which no one is allowed to be super-rich, one where everyone gets a more equal share of what is available: no private jets allowed, but better chances for people who are unfortunate. Human nature is like that: people tend to think of their own position when they describe a better world, whether they realize it or not. These prejudices and biases distort political thinking.

Rawls' stroke of genius was to come up with a thought experiment – he called it 'The Original Position' – that plays down some of the selfish biases we all have. His central idea is very simple: design a better society, but do it without knowing what position in society you'll occupy. You don't know whether you'll be rich, poor, have a disability, be good looking, male, female, ugly, intelligent or unintelligent, talented or unskilled, homosexual, bisexual or heterosexual. He thinks you will choose fairer principles behind this imaginary 'veil of ignorance' because you won't know where you might end up, what kind of a person you might be. From this simple device of choosing without knowing your own place, Rawls developed his theory of justice. This was based on two principles he thought all reasonable people would accept, principles of freedom and equality.

The first principle was his Liberty Principle. This states that everyone should have the right to a range of basic freedoms that mustn't be taken away from them, such as freedom of belief, freedom to vote for their leaders, and extensive freedom of expression. Even if restricting some of these freedoms improved the lives of a majority of people, Rawls thought, they were so important that the freedoms should be protected above all. Like all liberals, Rawls put a very high value on these basic liberties, believing that everyone had a right to them and that no one should take them away.

Rawls' second principle, the Difference Principle, is all about equality. Society should be arranged to give more equal wealth and opportunity to the most disadvantaged. If people receive different amounts of money, then this inequality is only allowed if it directly helps the worst off. A banker can only get 10,000 times more than the lowest-paid worker if the lowest-paid worker benefits directly and receives an increased amount of money that he or she wouldn't have had if the banker was paid less. If Rawls were in charge, no one would earn huge bonuses unless the poorest got more money as a result. Rawls thinks this is the kind of world reasonable people would choose if they didn't know whether they would be rich or poor themselves.

Before Rawls, philosophers and politicians who thought about who should get what often argued in favour of a situation which would produce the highest *average* amount of wealth. That could mean that some people could be super-rich, many moderately rich and few very poor. But for Rawls, such a situation was worse than one in which there were no super-rich, but everyone had a more equal share, even though the average amount of wealth was lower.

This is a challenging idea – particularly to those who are capable of earning high salaries in the world as it is. Robert Nozick (1938–2002), another important American political philosopher, further to the right politically than Rawls, questioned it. Surely fans who come to watch a brilliant basketball player should be free to give a small part of their ticket money to that player. It's their right to spend their money in this way. And if millions come to watch him, then the sportsman will – fairly, Nozick thought – earn millions of dollars. Rawls entirely disagreed with this view. Unless the poorest got richer as a result of this deal, Rawls argued, then the basketball player's personal earnings shouldn't be allowed to increase to such high levels. Rawls, controversially, believed that being a gifted athlete or a highly intelligent person did not automatically entitle individuals to higher earnings. That was in part because he believed that such things as sporting ability and intelligence were a matter of good luck. You don't deserve more simply because you are fortunate enough to be a fast runner or a great ball player, or if you are very bright. Being athletically talented or intelligent is the result of winning in the 'natural lottery'. Many people disagree strongly with Rawls and feel that excellence should be rewarded. But Rawls thought that there was no automatic connection between being good at something and deserving more.

But what if from behind the veil of ignorance some people would prefer to take a gamble? What if they thought of life as a lottery and wanted to make sure that there were some very attractive positions to occupy in society? Presumably gamblers might take the risk of ending up poor if they had a chance to be extremely rich. So they'd prefer a world with a wider range of economic possibilities than the one Rawls described. Rawls believed that reasonable people would not want to gamble with their lives in this way. Perhaps he was wrong about this.

For much of the twentieth century philosophers had lost touch with the great thinkers of the past. Rawls' *Theory of Justice* was one of the very few works of political philosophy written in that century that are worth mentioning in the same breath as those by Aristotle, Hobbes, Locke, Rousseau, Hume and Kant.

Rawls himself would have been far too modest to agree. His example, though, has inspired a generation of philosophers writing today, including Michael Sandel, Thomas Pogge, Martha Nussbaum and Will Kymlicka: they all believe that philosophy should engage with the deep and difficult questions about how we can and should live together. Unlike some philosophers of the previous generation, they aren't afraid of trying to answer them and to stimulate social change. They believe philosophy should actually change how we live, not just change how we discuss how we live.

Another philosopher who holds this kind of view is Peter Singer. He's the subject of the final chapter of this book. But before looking at his ideas, we are going to explore a question that is becoming more pertinent daily: 'Can Computers Think?'

CHAPTER 39

Can Computers Think?
ALAN TURING AND JOHN SEARLE

You're sitting in a room. There is a door into the room with a letterbox. Every now and then a piece of card with a squiggle shape drawn on it comes through the door and drops on your doormat. Your task is to look up the squiggle in a book that is on the table in the room. Each squiggle is paired with another symbol in the book. You have to find your squiggle in the book, look at the symbol it is paired with, and then find a bit of card with a symbol that matches it from a pack in the room. You then carefully push that bit of card out through your letterbox. That's it. You do this for a while and wonder what's going on.

This is the Chinese Room thought experiment, the invention of the American philosopher John Searle (born 1932). It's an imaginary situation designed to show that a computer can't really think even if it seems to. In order to see what's going on here you need to understand the Turing Test.

Alan Turing (1912–54) was an outstanding Cambridge mathematician who helped to invent the modern computer. His number-crunching machines built during the Second World War at Bletchley Park in England cracked the 'Enigma' codes used by German submarine commanders. The Allies could then intercept messages and know what the Nazis were planning.

Intrigued by the idea that one day computers might do more than crack codes, and could be genuinely intelligent, in 1950 he suggested a test that any such computer would have to pass. This has come to be known as the Turing Test for artificial intelligence but he originally called it the Imitation Game. It comes from his belief that what's interesting about the brain isn't that it has the consistency of cold porridge. Its function matters more than the way it wobbles when removed from the head, or the fact that it is grey. Computers may be hard and made from electronic components, but they can still do many things brains do.

When we judge whether a person is intelligent or not we do that based on the answers they give to questions rather than opening up their brains to look at how the neurons join up. So it's only fair that when we judge computers we focus on external evidence rather than on how they are constructed. We should look at inputs and outputs, not the blood and nerves or the wiring and transistors inside. Here's what Turing suggested. A tester is in one room, typing a conversation on to a screen. The tester doesn't know whether he or she is having a conversation with another person in a different room via the screen – or with a computer generating its own answers. If during the conversation the tester can't tell whether there is a person or a human being responding, the computer passes the Turing Test. If a computer passes that test then it is reasonable to say that it is intelligent – not just in a metaphorical way, but in the way that a human being can be.

What Searle's Chinese Room example – the scenario with the squiggles on bits of card – is meant to show is that even if a computer passed Turing's test for artificial intelligence that wouldn't prove that it genuinely understood anything. Remember you are in this room with strange symbols coming through the letterbox and are passing other symbols back out through the letterbox, and you are guided by a rulebook. This is a meaningless task for you, and you have no idea why you are doing it. But without your realizing it, you are answering questions in Chinese. You only speak English and know no Chinese at all. But the signs coming in are questions in Chinese, and the signs you give out are plausible answers to those questions. The Chinese Room with you in it wins the Imitation Game. You give answers that would fool someone outside into thinking that you really understand what you are talking about. So, this suggests, a computer that passes the Turing Test isn't necessarily intelligent, since from within the room you don't have any sense of what's being discussed at all.

Searle thinks that computers are like someone in the Chinese Room: they don't really have intelligence and can't really think. All they do is shuffle symbols around following rules that their makers have programmed into them. The processes they use are built into the software. But that is very different from truly understanding something or having genuine intelligence. Another way of putting this is that the people who program the computer give it a *syntax*: that is, they provide rules about the correct order in which to process the symbols. But they don't provide it with a *semantics*: they don't give *meanings* to the symbols. Human beings *mean* things when they speak – their thoughts relate in various ways to the world. Computers that seem to mean things are only imitating human thought, a bit like parrots. Although a parrot can mimic speech, it never really understands what it is saying. Similarly, according to Searle, computers don't really understand or think about anything: you can't get semantics from syntax alone.

A criticism of Searle's thought experiment is that it looks at the question of whether or not the person in the room understands what's going on. But that's a mistake. The person is just a part of the whole system. Even if the person doesn't understand what's going on, perhaps the whole system (including the room, the code book, the symbols and so on) understands. Searle's response to this objection was to change the thought experiment. Instead of imagining a person in a room shuffling symbols around, imagine this person has memorized the whole rulebook and then is outside in the middle of a field handing back the appropriate symbol cards. The person still wouldn't understand the individual questions even though he or she would give the right answers to the questions asked in Chinese. Understanding involves more than just giving the right answers.

Some philosophers, though, remain convinced that the human mind *is* just like a computer program. They believe that computers really can and do think. If they're right, then perhaps one day it will be possible to transfer minds from people's brains into computers. If your mind is a program, then just because it is running in the soggy mass of brain tissue in your head now doesn't mean that it couldn't run in a big shiny computer somewhere else in the future. If, with the help of super-intelligent computers, someone manages to map the billions of functional connections that make up your mind, then perhaps one day it will be possible to survive death. Your mind could be uploaded into a computer so that it could carry on working long after your body had been buried or cremated. Whether that would be a good way to exist is another question. If Searle is right, though, there would be no guarantee that the uploaded mind would be conscious in the way that you are now, even if it gave responses that seemed to show that it was.

Writing over sixty years ago, Turing was already convinced that computers could think. If he was right, it might not be that long before we find them thinking about philosophy. That's more likely than that they will allow our minds to survive death. Perhaps one day computers will even have interesting things to say about the fundamental questions of how we should live and about the nature of reality – the sorts of questions that philosophers have grappled with for several thousand years. In the meantime, though, we need to rely on flesh and blood philosophers to clarify our thinking in these areas. One of the most influential and controversial of these is Peter Singer.

CHAPTER 40

A Modern Gadfly
Peter Singer

You're in a garden where you know there is a pond. There's a splash and some shouting. You realize that a young child has fallen in and may be drowning. What do you do? Do you walk by? Even if you'd promised to meet a friend and stopping would make you late, you'd surely treat the child's life as more important than being on time. The pond is quite shallow, but very muddy. You'll ruin your best shoes if you help. But don't expect other people to understand if you don't jump in. This is about being human and valuing life. A child's life is so much more valuable than any pair of shoes, even a very expensive pair. Anyone who thinks otherwise is some kind of monster. You'd jump into the water, wouldn't you? Of course you would. But then you're also probably rich enough to prevent a child in Africa from dying of hunger or of a curable tropical disease. That probably wouldn't take much more than the price of the shoes you'd be prepared to ruin by saving the child in the pond.

Why haven't you helped the other children – assuming you haven't? Giving a small amount of money to the right charity would save at least one life. There are so many childhood diseases that can easily be prevented with a relatively small amount of money to pay for vaccinations and other medicines. But why don't you feel the same about someone dying in Africa as you do about a child you can see drowning in front of you? If you *do* feel the same, you are unusual. Most of us don't, even if we feel slightly awkward about that fact.

The Australian philosopher Peter Singer (born 1946) has argued that the drowning child in front of you and the starving child in Africa are not so different. We should care more about those we can save all over the world than we do. If we don't do something, then children who might otherwise have lived will certainly die young. This isn't a guess. We know it's true. We know that many thousands of children die each year from poverty-related causes. Some die of starvation while we in developed countries throw away food that rots in the fridge before we get round to eating it. Some can't even get clean water to drink. So we should give up one or two of the luxuries that we don't really need in order to help people who are unfortunate about where they were born. This is a hard philosophy to live up to. But that doesn't mean Singer is wrong about what we *ought* to do.

You might say that if you don't give money to charity, someone else probably will. The risk here is that we will all be like bystanders, each one assuming that someone else will do what is necessary. So many people across the world are living in extreme poverty and going to bed each day hungry that their need won't be met by leaving charity to the few. It is true that in the case of a child drowning in front of you it is very easy to see if someone else is coming to that child's aid. With those suffering in far-off countries it can be harder to know the effects of what we do and the effects of other people's actions. But that does not mean doing nothing is the best solution.

Connected with this point is the fear that giving money for overseas aid makes poor people depend on the rich, and stops them from finding ways to grow their own food and build their own wells and places to live. Over time this might make things turn out worse than if you didn't give at all. There are cases where whole countries have become dependent on foreign aid. What this means, though, is not that we should not contribute to charities, but that we should think carefully about the sorts of aid these charities are offering. It doesn't at all follow that we should not try and help. Some kinds of basic medical aid can give poor people a good chance of becoming independent of outside help. There are charities that are very good at training local people to help themselves, building wells that provide clean drinking water or providing health education. Singer's argument is not that we should simply contribute money to help others, but that we should contribute it to the charities that are most likely to benefit the worst off in the world in ways that will empower them to live independently. His message is clear: you almost certainly *could* have a genuine influence on other people's lives. And you *should*.

Singer is one of the best-known living philosophers. This is in part because he has challenged several widely held views. Some of what he believes is extremely controversial. Many people believe in the absolute sanctity of human life – that it is always wrong to kill another human being. Singer doesn't. If someone is in an irreversible persistent vegetative state, for example – that is, if they are just being kept alive as a body without meaningful conscious states or any chance of recovery or hope for their future – then Singer has argued that euthanasia or mercy killing may be appropriate. There is little point in keeping such people alive in this state, he believes, as they have no capacity for pleasure or for any preference about how they live. They don't have a strong wish to keep on living, because they are incapable of having wishes at all.

Such views have made him unpopular in some quarters. He has even been called a Nazi for defending euthanasia in these special circumstances – despite the fact that his parents were Viennese Jews who fled the Nazis. This name-calling refers to the fact that the Nazis killed many thousands of sick and physically and mentally disabled people on the grounds that their lives were allegedly not worth living. It would be wrong to call the Nazi programme 'mercy killing' or 'euthanasia', however, since it was not meant to prevent unnecessary suffering, but to get rid of those the Nazis dismissed as 'useless mouths' because they were unable to work, and because they were supposedly contaminating the Aryan race. There was no sense of 'mercy' there. In contrast Singer is interested in the quality of life of the people concerned, and would certainly never have supported to any degree the Nazis' policies – though some of his opponents caricature his views to make them sound very similar.

Singer first became famous because of his influential books about the treatment of animals, especially *Animal Liberation*, which was published in 1975. In the early nineteenth century Jeremy Bentham had argued for the need to take animal suffering seriously, but in the 1970s when Singer first began writing on this topic, few philosophers saw it this way. Singer, like Bentham and Mill (see Chapters 21 and 24), is a consequentialist. This means he believes that the best action is the one that produces the best result. And to work out the best result we need to take into account what is in the best interests of all concerned, including the interests of animals. Like Bentham,

Singer believes that the key relevant feature for most animals is their capacity to feel pain. As human beings, we sometimes experience greater suffering than an animal would in a similar situation because we have the ability to reason and understand what is happening to us. This too needs to be taken into account.

Singer called those who don't give enough weight to the interests of animals 'speciesist'. This is like being racist or sexist. Racists treat members of their own race differently: they give them special treatment. They don't give members of other races what they deserve. A white racist might, for example, give a job to another white person even though there is a better-qualified black person who applied for the job. That's clearly unfair and wrong. Speciesism is like racism. It comes from only seeing your own species' perspective or being very heavily biased in its favour. As human beings many of us think only of other human beings when we decide what to do. But that's wrong. Animals can suffer, and their suffering should be taken into account.

Giving equal respect doesn't mean treating every animal species in exactly the same way. That wouldn't make sense at all. If you slap a horse across the rump with an open hand you probably won't cause the horse much pain. Horses have thick skins. But if you did the same to a human baby, you would cause it intense pain. But if you hit the horse hard enough to cause the horse the same amount of pain as slapping a baby would, that would be just as morally wrong as slapping a baby. You shouldn't do either, of course.

Singer argues that we should all be vegetarians on the grounds that we can easily live well without eating animals. Most food production using animals causes suffering and some farming is so cruel that it causes the animals intense pain. Factory-farmed chickens, for example, are kept in tiny cages, some pigs are reared in stalls so small they can't turn round, and the process of slaughtering cattle is often extremely distressing and painful for them. It can't, Singer argued, be morally right to let such farming continue. But even more humane forms of farming animals are unnecessary, as we can quite easily do without eating meat. True to his principles, he even printed a recipe for lentil daal in one of his books to encourage readers to seek alternatives to meat.

Farm animals aren't the only ones that suffer at the hands of human beings. Scientists use animals for their research. It's not just rats and guinea pigs – cats, dogs, monkeys and even chimpanzees can be found in laboratories, many of them suffering pain and distress as they are drugged or given electric shocks. Singer's test to see if any research is morally acceptable is this: would we be prepared to perform the same experiment on a brain-damaged human being? If not, he believes, it is not right to perform the experiment on an animal with a similar level of mental awareness. This is a tough test, and not many experiments would pass it. In practice, then, Singer is very strongly against using animals in research.

The whole of Singer's approach to moral questions is based on the idea of consistency. Consistency is treating similar cases in a similar way. It is a matter of logic that if what is wrong with harming human beings is that it causes pain, then other animals' pain should affect how we behave too. If harming an animal brings about more pain than harming a human being, then it's better to harm the human being if you have to harm one of them.

Like Socrates many years before him, Singer takes risks when he makes public statements about how we should live. There have been protests against some of his lectures and he has had death threats. Yet he represents the very best tradition in philosophy. He is constantly challenging widely held assumptions. His philosophy affects how he lives, and when he disagrees with other people he is always prepared to challenge the opinions of those he finds around him, to engage in public discussion.

Most importantly, Singer supports his conclusions with reasoned arguments informed by well-researched facts. You don't have to agree with his conclusions to see his sincerity as a philosopher. Philosophy, after all, thrives on debate. It thrives on people taking positions against each other and arguing, using logic and evidence. If you disagree with Singer's views on, for example, the moral status of animals or the circumstances in which euthanasia is morally acceptable, there is still a very good chance that reading his books will make you think hard about what you do actually believe and how it is supported by facts, reasons and principles.

Philosophy began with awkward questions and difficult challenges; with gadfly philosophers like Peter Singer around, there is a good chance that the spirit of Socrates will continue to shape its future.

Index